CODI-CRAC Shared Task on Anaphora, Bridging, and Discourse Deixis in Dialogue (CODI-CRAC 2022)

Held at COLING 2022

Gyeongju, South Korea
17 October 2022

ISBN: 978-1-7138-6149-2

Printed from e-media with permission by:

Curran Associates, Inc.
57 Morehouse Lane
Red Hook, NY 12571

Some format issues inherent in the e-media version may also appear in this print version.

Printed with permission by Curran Associates, Inc. (2023)

For permission requests, please contact the Association for Computational Linguistics at the address below.

Association for Computational Linguistics
209 N. Eighth Street
Stroudsburg, Pennsylvania 18360

Phone: 1-570-476-8006
Fax: 1-570-476-0860

acl@aclweb.org

Additional copies of this publication are available from:

Curran Associates, Inc.
57 Morehouse Lane
Red Hook, NY 12571 USA
Phone: 845-758-0400
Fax: 845-758-2633
Email: curran@proceedings.com
Web: www.proceedings.com

COLING

Volume 29 (2022), No. 2

Proceedings of the CODI-CRAC 2022 Shared Task on Anaphora, Bridging, and Discourse Deixis in Dialogue (CODI-CRAC 2022)

The 29th International Conference on Computational Linguistics

October 17, 2022
Gyeongju, Republic of Korea

ISSN 2951-2093

Message from the Program Co-Chairs

This shared task, the second of two so far, represents the collaborative efforts of a diverse team of researchers, across countries, institutional types, research areas, and career stages. The idea for this series of share tasks emerged through a Discourse Analysis breakout session at SIGDIAL 2020. The goal was to foster a more active partnership between the discourse and dialogue communities and to offer, not just a competition, but an opportunity to identify the next great challenges for the area of coreference.

Since that initial discussion at the Spring 2020 conference, the core organizing team has met almost weekly to build a vision for this shared task as the initial event out of what is hoped to become a series of such events, and situated in partnership with other related efforts, such as the Universal Anaphora effort. In the past year, in order to support an expansion of the initial annotation effort, the team has added an additional member, Lori Levin from the Language Technologies Institute at Carnegie Mellon University.

The team is excited to host this shared task, this year co-located with COLING 2022. Each of the organizing team's members are also grateful to their respective institutions for providing the kind of environment that facilitates such international collaborations. The team is grateful for funding committed by the Heidelberg Institute for Theoretical Studies, the Dali Project at Queen Mary University and the Language Technologies Institute at Carnegie Mellon University (all of which supported annotation for this series of shared task events) as well as resources provided by Intel (especially in connection with the CODALAB infrastructure). The annotation team managed jointly for this shared task by Queen Mary University and Carnegie Mellon University worked tirelessly to produce the annotated data, without which this shared task would not be a shared task at all! The team is also grateful for the synergistic efforts of the broader ACL community, for providing an environment in which the vision for this shared task could be realized and situated within this vibrant COLING milieu.

Organizing Committee

- Juntao Yu, University of Essex, UK
- Sopan Khosla, Amazon, USA
- Ramesh Manuvinakurike, Intel, USA
- Lori Levin , Carnegie Mellon University, USA
- Vincent Ng, University of Texas at Dallas, USA
- Massimo Poesio, Queen Mary University, UK
- Michael Strube, Heidelberg Institute for Theoretical Studies, Germany
- Carolyn Rose, Carnegie Mellon University, USA

Table of Contents

CODI-CRAC Shared Task Program

Monday October 17, 2022

14:00–15:30 Session 1: Shared Task Competition

14:00 Welcome

14:05 *The CODI-CRAC 2022 Shared Task on Anaphora, Bridging, and Discourse Deixis in Dialogue*
Juntao Yu, Sopan Khosla, Ramesh Manuvinakurike, Lori Levin, Vincent Ng, Massimo Poesio, Michael Strube and Carolyn Rosé

14:35 *Anaphora Resolution in Dialogue: System Description (CODI-CRAC 2022 Shared Task)*
Tatiana Anikina, Natalia Skachkova, Joseph Renner and Priyansh Trivedi

14:50 *Pipeline Coreference Resolution Model for Anaphoric Identity in Dialogues*
Damrin Kim, Seongsik Park, Mirae Han and Harksoo Kim

15:05 *Neural Anaphora Resolution in Dialogue Revisited*
Shengjie Li, Hideo Kobayashi and Vincent Ng

15:30–16:00 Coffee Break

16:00–18:00 Session 2: Keynote Session

Monday October 17, 2022 (continued)

16:00 **Invited Talk: Massimo Poesio and Lori Levin**

16:45 **Open Discussion**

17:45 **Closing Remarks**

The CODI-CRAC 2022 Shared Task on Anaphora, Bridging, and Discourse Deixis in Dialogue

Juntao Yu[1], **Sopan Khosla**[2]*, **Ramesh Manuvinakurike**[3], **Lori Levin**[4], **Vincent Ng**[5], **Massimo Poesio**[6], **Michael Strube**[7], and **Carolyn Rosé**[4]
[1]Univ. of Essex, UK; [2]AWS AI, Amazon, USA [3]Intel Labs, USA; [4]Canegie Mellon Univ., USA
[5]UT Dallas, USA; [6]Queen Mary Univ., UK; [7]HITS, Germany;
j.yu@essex.ac.uk; sopankh@amazon.com; ramesh.manuvinakurike@intel.com; levin@andrew.cmu.edu; vince@hlt.utdallas.edu; m.poesio@qmul.ac.uk; Michael.Strube@h-its.org; cprose@cs.cmu.edu

Abstract

The CODI-CRAC 2022 Shared Task on Anaphora Resolution in Dialogues is the second edition of an initiative focused on detecting different types of anaphoric relations in conversations of different kinds. Using five conversational datasets, four of which have been newly annotated with a wide range of anaphoric relations: identity, bridging references and discourse deixis, we defined multiple tasks focusing individually on these key relations. The second edition of the shared task maintained the focus on these relations and used the same datasets as in 2021, but new test data were annotated, the 2021 data were checked, and new subtasks were added. In this paper, we discuss the annotation schemes, the datasets, the evaluation scripts used to assess the system performance on these tasks, and provide a brief summary of the participating systems and the results obtained across 230 runs from three teams, with most submissions achieving significantly better results than our baseline methods.

1 Introduction

The performance of models for single-antecedent anaphora resolution on the aspects of anaphoric interpretation annotated in the standard ONTONOTES dataset (Pradhan et al., 2012) has greatly improved in recent years (Wiseman et al., 2015; Lee et al., 2017, 2018; Kantor and Globerson, 2019; Joshi et al., 2020). So the attention of the community has started to turn to more complex cases of anaphora not found or not properly tested in ONTONOTES, and on genres other than news.

Well-known examples of this trend are work on the cases of anaphora whose interpretation requires some form of commonsense knowledge tested by benchmarks for the Winograd Schema Challenge (Rahman and Ng, 2012; Liu et al., 2017; Sakaguchi et al., 2020), or the pronominal anaphors that cannot be resolved purely using gender, for which benchmarks such as GAP have been developed (Webster et al., 2018). GAP, however, still focused on identity coreference. In addition, more research has been carried out on aspects of anaphoric interpretation that go beyond identity anaphora but are covered by datasets such as ARRAU (Poesio et al., 2018; Uryupina et al., 2020). These include, e.g., bridging reference (Clark, 1977; Hou et al., 2018; Hou, 2020; Yu and Poesio, 2020; Kobayashi and Ng, 2021), discourse deixis (Webber, 1991; Marasović et al., 2017; Kolhatkar et al., 2018) or split-antecedent anaphora (Eschenbach et al., 1989; Vala et al., 2016; Zhou and Choi, 2018; Yu et al., 2020b, 2021).

There has also been interest in other genres apart from news. This includes substantial research on annotating and resolving coreference in biomedical and other scientific domains (Cohen et al., 2017; Lu and Poesio, 2021) as well as in literary documents (Bamman et al., 2020). There are, however, language genres still understudied in the literature on anaphoric reference. Arguably the most important among these is conversational language in dialogue. Anaphora resolution in dialogue requires systems to handle grammatically incorrect language suffering from disfluencies and mentions jointly created across utterances (Poesio and Rieser, 2010) or whose function is to establish common ground rather than refer (Clark and Brennan, 1990; Heeman and Hirst, 1995). Dialogue involves much more deictic reference, vaguer anaphoric and discourse deictic reference, speaker grounding of pronouns and long-distance conversation structure. These are complexities that are normally absent from news or Wikipedia articles, which constitute the bulk of current datasets for coreference resolution (Poesio et al., 2016). There has been some research on coreference in dialogue (Byron, 2002; Eckert and Strube, 2001; Müller, 2008), but very limited in scope (primarily related to pronominal interpretation), due to the lack of suitable corpora.

*Work was done prior to joining AWS AI Labs.

Proceedings of the CODI-CRAC 2022 Shared Task on Anaphora, Bridging, and Discourse Deixis in Dialogue, pages 1–14
Gyeongju, Republic of Korea, October 17, 2022. ©2022 Association for Computational Linguistics
https://doi.org/10.26615/978-954-452-056-4_001

The one language for which substantial corpora of coreference in dialogue exist is French: the ANCOR corpus (Muzerelle et al., 2014) has enabled the development of an end-to-end neural model for coreference interpretation in dialogue by Grobol (2020). For English, the one resource we are aware of fully annotated for anaphoric reference is the TRAINS corpora included in the ARRAU corpus (Uryupina et al., 2020).

The CODI-CRAC 2021 Shared Task in Anaphora Resolution in Dialogue (Khosla et al., 2021) was organized to address this need for datasets about anaphoric reference in dialogue by providing participants with the opportunity to develop automated approaches for anaphora resolution that tackle less studied forms of anaphora as well as coreference, and generalize to different types of conversational setups. A number of groups participated to this first edition, but we organizers also realised that the community could benefit from a second edition using more data and more cleaned-up, adding more tasks, and improving the evaluation. As a result, we organized this year's second edition. [1] Like the first edition, CODI-CRAC 2022 involved three tasks that individually tackle a particular anaphoric relation: identity, bridging, and discourse deixis, in four conversational datasets from different domains newly annotated with the above-mentioned relations. Unlike the first edition, participants also had training data in those four domains, in addition to development and test sets. To accommodate for systems that use gold/predicted mentions for bridging and discourse deixis tasks, we set up separate leaderboards for the two settings.

In this paper wepresent an overview of the CODI-CRAC 2022 shared task. We begin by providing some background in Section 2 and introducing the new CODI-CRAC 2022 corpus in Section 3. We then provide an extensive overview of the different CODI-CRAC 2022 tasks, markable settings, and evaluation metrics in Section 4, and submission details in Section 5. This is followed by details of the baselines in Section 6 and participating systems in Section 7. We present a discussion of the performance of the systems on different tasks and sub-corpora in Section 8, and finally conclude this paper in Section 9.

[1] https://codalab.lisn.upsaclay.fr/competitions/614

2 Background

2.1 Beyond Identity Coreference

Most modern anaphoric annotation projects cover basic identity anaphora as in (1).

(1) [Mary]$_i$ bought [a new dress]$_j$ but [it]$_j$ didn't fit [her]$_i$.

However, many other types of identity anaphora exist, as well as other types of anaphoric relations that are not annotated in ONTONOTES but are annotated in other corpora. The CODI-CRAC 2021 and 2022 Shared Tasks covered the range of anaphoric relations included in the first Universal Anaphora survey of phenomena to be covered (see below)

Split-antecedent anaphora **Split-antecedent anaphors** (Eschenbach et al., 1989; Kamp and Reyle, 1993) are cases of plural identity reference to sets composed of two or more entities introduced by separate noun phrases, as in (2).

(2) [John]$_1$ met [Mary]$_2$. [He]$_1$ greeted [her]$_2$. [They]$_{1,2}$ went to the movies.

Such references are annotated in, e.g., ARRAU (Uryupina et al., 2020), GUM (Zeldes, 2017) and *Phrase Detectives* (Poesio et al., 2019).

Discourse deixis In ONTONOTES, **event anaphora**, a subtype of **discourse deixis** (Webber, 1991; Kolhatkar et al., 2018) is marked, as in (3) (where *[that]* arguably refers to the event of a white rabbit with pink ears running past Alice) but not the whole range of abstract anaphora, illustrated by, e.g., *[this]* in the same example, which refers to the fact that the Rabbit was able to talk. (Both examples from the *Phrase Detectives* corpus (Poesio et al., 2019).)

(3) So she was considering in her own mind (as well as she could, for the hot day made her feel very sleepy and stupid), whether the pleasure of making a daisy-chain would be worth the trouble of getting up and picking the daisies, when suddenly a White Rabbit with pink eyes ran close by her. There was nothing so VERY remarkable in [that]; nor did Alice think it so VERY much out of the way to hear the Rabbit say to itself, 'Oh dear! Oh dear! I shall be late!' (when she thought it over afterwards, it occurred to her that she ought to have wondered at

this, but at the time it all seemed quite natural); but when the Rabbit actually TOOK A WATCH OUT OF ITS WAISTCOAT-POCKET, and looked at it, and then hurried on, Alice started to her feet, for it flashed across her mind that she had never before seen a rabbit with either a waistcoat-pocket, or a watch to take out of it, and burning with curiosity, she ran across the field after it, and fortunately was just in time to see it pop down a large rabbit-hole under the hedge.

Bridging references There are other forms of anaphoric reference besides identity, and there are now a number of corpora annotating (a subset of) these forms. Possibly the most studied of non-identity anaphora is **bridging reference** or **associative anaphora** (Clark, 1977; Hawkins, 1978; Prince, 1981) as in (4), where bridging reference / associative anaphora *the roof* refers to an object which is related to / associated with, but not identical to, the *hall*.

(4) There was not a moment to be lost: away went Alice like the wind, and was just in time to hear it say, as it turned a corner, 'Oh my ears and whiskers, how late it's getting!' She was close behind it when she turned the corner, but the Rabbit was no longer to be seen: she found herself in [a long, low hall, which was lit up by a row of lamps hanging from [the roof]].

2.2 Universal Anaphora

The more general types of anaphoric reference just discussed are now routinely annotated in a number of corpora, including ANCORA (Recasens and Martí, 2010), ARRAU (Uryupina et al., 2020), GNOME (Poesio, 2004), GUM (Zeldes, 2017), ISNOTES (Markert et al., 2012), the Prague Dependency Treebank (Nedoluzhko, 2013), and TÜBA-DZ (Versley, 2008). (See Poesio et al. (2016) for a more detailed survey and Nedoluzhko et al. (2021) for a more recent, extensive update.)

Some of these resources are of a sufficient size to support shared tasks. In particular, the ARRAU corpus was used as the dataset for the Shared Task on Anaphora Resolution with ARRAU in the CRAC 2018 Workshop (Poesio et al., 2018).

In order to enable further progress in the empirical study of anaphora by coordinating the many existing efforts to annotate not just identity coreference, but all aspects of anaphoric interpretation from identity of sense anaphora to bridging to discourse deixis; and not just for English, but all languages, the **Universal Anaphora** (UA) initiative was launched in 2020.[2] Progress so far includes a first proposal concerning the range of phenomena to be covered, as well as a survey of the range of existing anaphoric annotations and a proposal for a markup format extending the CONLL-U format developed by the **Universal Dependencies** initiative[3] with mechanisms for marking up the range of anaphoric information covered by UA. Crucially, a scorer able to evaluate all types of anaphoric reference in the scope of the proposal was also developed, which was used in CODI-CRAC 2021 and for this shared task (Yu et al., 2022).

2.3 Datasets of Anaphora in Dialogue

A limitation of most resources annotated for anaphora is that they mostly focus on expository text. The one substantial dataset of anaphoric relations in dialogue is ANCOR for French (Muzerelle et al., 2014), in which identity and bridging anaphora are annotated. Among the small number of English corpora that cover dialogue include ONTONOTES (Pradhan et al., 2012), which contains a small number of conversations annotated for identity anaphora and a small subtype of discourse deixis (as discussed earlier). ARRAU's (Poesio and Artstein, 2008; Uryupina et al., 2020) TRAINS sub-corpus consists of task-oriented dialogues for identity, bridging, and discourse deixis. We include TRAINS in CODI-CRAC 2022 training data. The more recently released ONTOGUM (Zhu et al., 2021) builds upon the ONTONOTES schema and adds several new genres (including more spoken data) to the ONTONOTES family. Both identity anaphora and bridging are annotated in the dataset.

3 The CODI-CRAC 2022 Corpus

One of the objectives of the CODI-CRAC shared tasks was to annotate new data for studying anaphora in dialogue. The only existing dataset covering the full range of phenomena and with some coverage of dialogue, the ARRAU data used for the CRAC 2018 Shared Task, was made available as training material. In addition, new data

[2]https://universalanaphora.github.io/UniversalAnaphora/

[3]https://universaldependencies.org/

from dialogue corpora were annotated for development and testing using the same annotation scheme used in ARRAU.

3.1 ARRAU: Corpus and Annotation Scheme

Genres The ARRAU corpus[4] (Poesio and Artstein, 2008; Uryupina et al., 2020) was designed to cover a variety of genres. It includes a substantial amount of news text in a sub-corpus called RST, consisting of the Penn Treebank (Marcus et al., 1993). The TRAINS domain of task-oriented dialogues includes a complete annotation of the TRAINS-93 corpus[5] and the pilot dialogues in the so-called TRAINS-91 corpus. In addition, ARRAU includes a complete annotation of the spoken narratives in the Pear Stories (Chafe, 1980), and documents in the medical and art history genres from the GNOME corpus (Poesio, 2004).

Annotation scheme Following the CRAC 2018 shared task, a revised version of the annotation guidelines was produced, as part of the work on the ARRAU 3 release of the corpus. The new annotation guidelines were completed after CODI-CRAC 2021 and made available on the corpus page.[6] The new guidelines were used in CODI-CRAC 2022 to check the annotation of the documents already annotated for CODI-CRAC 2021 and to annotate new data. For more information on the scheme, please consult the manual or, for a quick summary, (Khosla et al., 2021).

3.2 New Data

The annotated corpus created for CODI-CRAC 2022 consists of conversations from the same well-known conversational datasets already used in CODI-CRAC 2021: the AMI corpus (Carletta, 2006), the LIGHT corpus (Urbanek et al., 2019), the PERSUASION corpus (Wang et al., 2019) and SWITCHBOARD (Godfrey et al., 1992). For each of these datasets, documents for about 15K tokens were annotated in 2021 for development according to the ARRAU annotation scheme, and about the same number of tokens were annotated for testing. For this year's shared task, the development data from 2021 were used as training data; the test data from 2021 were used as development data; and new test data were annotated.

Switchboard SWITCHBOARD[7] (Godfrey et al., 1992) is one of the best known dialogue corpora. It consists of 1,155 five-minute spontaneous telephone conversations between two participants not previously acquainted with each other. In these conversations, callers question receivers on provided topics, such as child care, recycling, and news media. 440 speakers participate in these 1,155 conversations, producing 221,616 utterances. It was annotated for dialogue acts by Stolcke et al. (1997)[8] and for information status by Nissim et al. (2004).

AMI The AMI corpus[9] (Carletta, 2006) is a collection of 100 hours of meeting recordings between several participants. The recordings include signals from close-talking and far-field microphones, individual and room-view video cameras, and output from a slide projector and an electronic whiteboard. Several types of annotation were carried out, including dialogue acts, topics, summaries, named entities, and focus of attention.

Light Amazon, Facebook, Google, and other AI companies have all created dialogue corpora in recent years to support their research on conversational agents. LIGHT (Urbanek et al., 2019) is one of the many recently created corpora available on the `Parl.ai` platform.[10] LIGHT is a large-scale fantasy text adventure game research platform for training agents that can both talk and act, interacting either with other models or with humans. The LIGHT corpus was entirely created through crowdsourcing at different levels. In the first round, workers created a number of settings (the King's palace, the dark forest, etc); then in a second round workers created fitting characters for each scenario, providing information about their background history, their personality, etc. Finally, in a third round, workers created dialogues between these characters.

[4] http://www.arrauproject.org

[5] http://www.ldc.upenn.edu/Catalog/catalogEntry.jsp?catalogId=LDC95S25

[6] https://github.com/arrauproject/data/blob/main/ARRAU_3_Annotation_Manual_1.0.pdf

[7] https://catalog.ldc.upenn.edu/LDC97S62

[8] This version is available from https://convokit.cornell.edu/documentation/switchboard.html

[9] https://groups.inf.ed.ac.uk/ami/corpus/

[10] https://parl.ai/projects/light/

Persuasion The Persuasion for Good corpus[11] (Wang et al., 2019) is a collection of online conversations generated by Amazon Mechanical Turk workers, where one participant (the persuader) tries to convince the other (the persuadee) to donate to a charity. 1017 conversations were collected in total, along with demographic data and responses to psychological surveys from users. Several speaker-level annotations were marked, including, e.g., demographics, the big five personality traits, etc.

3.3 Annotation

The dataset was annotated using the same MMAX2 tool (Müller and Strube, 2006) – indeed, almost exactly the same MMAX style – used to annotate and check ARRAU Release 2 and Release 3. But this time, the annotation work was divided between the DALI team at Queen Mary University (Maris Camilleri and Paloma Carretero Garcia, who have been annotating ARRAU 3), and a team at CMU coordinated by Lori Levin (Taiqi He and Katherine Zhang). This division of labor made it possible to (i) ensure that every new document would be annotated by at least two annotators, (ii) re-check the documents already annotated in 2021, and (iii) test the reliability of the scheme.

3.4 The Corpus

Some basic statistics about the CODI-CRAC 2022 dataset are provided in Table 1. For each dataset, the Table reports number of documents, size in tokens, number of markables, and how many of these are Discourse Old (Identity Coreference) anaphors (DO), bridging references, and discourse deixis. With a total of 214,625 tokens and 60,993, the CODI-CRAC 2022 dataset is to our knowledge the largest dataset annotated for anaphoric interpretation in dialogue. It is also one of the largest datasets annotated for bridging references.

After annotation, the documents were converted into the CONLL-UA 'Extended' format used by the scorer, described by a document on the Universal Anaphora site.[12]

AMI, LIGHT and PERSUASION are freely available from the Shared Task Codalab site. ARRAU and SWITCHBOARD are distributed by LDC.[13]

[11] https://convokit.cornell.edu/documentation/persuasionforgood.html

[12] https://github.com/UniversalAnaphora/UniversalAnaphora/blob/main/documents/UA_CONLL_U_Plus_proposal_v1.0.md

[13] ARRAU is also freely available to any group that purchased the Penn Treebank and TRAINS-93 corpora from LDC.

4 Task Description

Following the structure of the last year's Shared Task, CODI-CRAC 2022 covers three key aspects of anaphoric interpretation: identity anaphora, bridging anaphora, and discourse deixis. Participants or groups could participate in one or more tasks.

4.1 Markable Settings

To address the challenge of the bridging reference resolution and discourse deixis tasks, in addition to the predicted (Pred) and gold mention (Gold M) settings from last year, a gold anaphors (Gold A) setting is added to those tasks. In total, the Bridging (Task2) and Discourse Deixis (Task 3) tasks have three settings: Pred: the system is responsible for predicting their mentions; Gold M: with the gold mentions provided and Gold A: both gold anaphors and gold mentions were provided. The three settings were run in the order of Pred, Gold M and Gold A – the later settings became available after the runs under the previous settings had been submitted. The three settings were scored separately and independently.

4.2 Evaluation Settings

Same as last year, the Universal Anaphora (UA) scorer (Yu et al., 2022; Paun et al., 2022) was used to evaluate the systems. The same settings for last year's shared task were used, more specifically, the settings for the individual tasks are as follows:[14]

Task 1 For Task 1, we use the default settings of the scorer where the identity relations (including split-antecedents) and singletons were evaluated. Non-referring expressions were excluded from the evaluation.

```
python ua-scorer.py key system
```

Task 2 For Task 2, the scorer was called using the following command:

```
python ua-scorer.py key system \
    keep_bridging
```

Task 3 Finally, for Task 3, the scorer was called using the following command.

```
python ua-scorer.py key system \
    evaluate_discourse_deixis
```

[14] For a full description of the task(s), see https://github.com/juntaoy/codi-crac2022_scripts/blob/main/2022_CODI_CRAC_Introduction.md

		Docs	Tokens	Markables	DO	Bridging	Disc. Deix
LIGHT	train	20	11495	3907	2132	381	72
	dev	21	11824	3941	2181	424	84
	test	38	22017	7330	3770	812	128
AMI	train	7	33741	8918	4579	853	230
	dev	3	18260	4870	2350	638	118
	test	3	16562	3990	2007	432	118
PERSUASION	train	21	9185	2743	1242	248	95
	dev	27	12198	3697	1715	316	133
	test	33	14719	4233	2111	304	105
SWITCHBOARD	train	11	14992	4024	1679	589	128
	dev	22	35027	9392	3991	1165	265
	test	12	14605	3888	1606	464	107
Total		218	214625	60933	29363	6626	1583

Table 1: Statistics about the CODI-CRAC 2022 corpus (new datasets only)

5 Submission Details

The shared task was hosted on a single CodaLab page, including evaluations and datasets distribution. The competition consists of three development phases and seven evaluation phases. In the development phases, a small in-domain training set for each domain alongside a large out-of-domain training set (i.e. the ARRAU corpus) is available. In addition, a validation set for each domain is also provided. The development phases are handy tools to get the systems prepared for the evaluation phases. Apart from the development phases, the participants can also download the scoring script to evaluate their systems offline. During the evaluation phases, the different versions of the unseen test sets (Pred, Gold M, Gold A) were released incrementally to accommodate the needs of the evaluation phases. The submissions were evaluated individually on each of the four domains, and then the macro-average of the four scores are used for the final ranking of individual tasks. Apart from the corpora provided by us, additional resources were also permitted.

6 Baselines

We used the same baseline systems from last year's shared task, and further, evaluate those baselines in the newly introduced phases. More precisely the baselines for identity anaphora and bridging reference resolution tasks are derived from state-of-the-art neural models, whereas the discourse deixis baseline is a simple but effective system based on heuristic rules.

For identity anaphora resolution (Task 1), we used the coreference resolution model provided by the Xu and Choi (2020)[15]. More specifically, we use their SpanBERT setting without any higher-order inference (SpanBERT + no HOI), The model was trained with the ONTONOTES (English) dataset and then evaluated directly on CODI-CRAC 2022 datasets without fine-tuning.

For bridging reference resolution (Task 2), we use the single-task variant of the Yu and Poesio (2020) system[16]. The system is trained on the bridging annotations of the RST sub-corpus of ARRAU. Since the system do not predict the mentions itself, for the predicted mention setting (Pred), we supply the system with mentions predicted by Yu et al. (2020a)'s mention detector (BIAFFINE MD)[17]. The mention detector was also trained on the same RST sub-corpus of ARRAU. For Gold M and Gold A settings, we use the gold mentions and anaphoras provided respectively. The system is evaluated on CODI-CRAC 2022 data without further training.

For discourse deixis (Task 3), the baseline for predicted mention setting (Pred) uses two simple heuristics: first only considers demonstrative pronouns (*this*, *that*) as anaphors and then uses the immediately preceding clause/utterance in the conver-

[15]`https://github.com/lxucs/coref-hoi/`
[16]`https://github.com/juntaoy/dali-bridging`
[17]`https://github.com/juntaoy/dali-md`

sation to be their antecedent. For the gold mention setting (Gold M) we further restrict the anaphors to be the intersection of the demonstrative pronouns and the gold mentions and then apply the same rule for antecedent selection. For the gold anaphor setting (Gold A), the baseline links the gold anaphors to their immediately preceding clause/utterance. The heuristic-based baselines are then evaluated on the CODI-CRAC 2022 data of all four domains.

The performance of our baselines on different sub-corpora is shown in Tables 3, 4, and 5 alongside the participant systems.

A helper script developed from last year's shared task is available to help participants convert the CONLL-UA format to and back from the various JSON format used by our baselines[18].

7 Participating Systems

Similar to last year, a total of 54 individual participants registered for the CODI-CRAC 2022 shared task on CodaLab. Among them, three teams submitted results for Task 1, and two submitted results for Task 2 and Task 3. Apart from Emory_NLP, all the teams from last year participated in this year's shared task, but DFKI and INRIA joined forces to participate as one team. All three teams (UTD_NLP, KU_NLP, DFKI-INRIA) submitted system description papers. We summarize their approaches below and in Table 2.

UTD_NLP participated in all three tasks. For identity anaphora, the authors built a pipeline system consisting of three components: a mention detector, an entity coreference resolver and a non-referring/entity classifier. All three components use the same underlining system they used in last year's shared task (Kobayashi et al., 2021), a multi-task learning approach adapted from the Xu and Choi (2020) system for mention detector and coreference resolution. The training objectives and priorities, however, were configured differently to maximise the performance of the individual tasks. Finally, those components were used in a pipeline fashion to deliver their final results. For discourse deixis, a system similar to Xu and Choi (2020)'s was used. They use both heuristics and a binary classifier to supply the anaphors. For each anaphor, antecedents were selected from up to 10 immediate previous utterances. The team based their bridging resolution system on the Yu and Poesio (2020)'s model, with additional dialogue-specific features included. The main focus of this year was on exploring the different pre-training and fine-tuning strategy. In total, four different training strategies were evaluated by them..

KU_NLP submitted results for identity anaphora resolution (task 1). The team proposed a pipeline system that resolves the mentions separately from the coreference resolution. The mention detection part solves the problem by classifying all possible mentions into mentions and non-mentions. The predicted mentions then feed into the coreference part of the system that solves the task in a mention-pair fashion. Additional speaker features were used to leverage the mention representations.

DFKI-INRIA participated in all three tasks. For the identity anaphora task, they utilise the Workspace Coreference System (WCS) (Anikina et al., 2021) they introduced in last year's shared task with the Xu and Choi (2020) system. The singletons predicted by the WCS system are added to the Xu and Choi (2020) to create their final results. Similar to the WCS system, the mentions are predicted separately using SpaCy. For bridging, they build their system on a simplified Joshi et al. (2019) system with mention pruning and coarse-to-fine steps removed. They only submitted to the Gold A phase, where gold mentions and gold anaphors were provided. For discourse deixis, the team employ a multi-task learning approach based on the Xu and Choi (2020) system, the system first uses heuristics to find the candidate anaphors, then resolve the antecedents and finally uses an anaphora type classifier to filter out the identity, non-referring anaphors. The system also used several linguistic features (e.g. PoS, dependency relations) to aid the anaphora type classification.

8 Results and Discussion

8.1 Task 1 – Identity Anaphora

All three teams participated the task 1, in total they made 55 runs to the official leaderboard. For this task, we report the CoNLL average F1 scores for each sub-corpus and take the macro-average of them to rank the participating systems.

As shown in Table 3, all the participating systems outperform the baseline by large margins (up to 27% on the macro-average scores). The best result was achieved by the UTD_NLP team, with large improvements over the baseline by more than

[18]https://github.com/juntaoy/codi-crac2022_scripts

Track	Team	Baselines	Framework	Markable ID	Train. Data	Dev. Data
Anaphora Resolution	UTD_NLP	Xu and Choi (2020)	A pipeline of mention detection, entity coreference and non-referring/mention removal components. Modifies baseline to handle singleton clusters and enforce dialogue-specific constraints.	Adapted from Xu and Choi (2020)	CODI-CRAC 2022 + OntoNotes	CODI-CRAC 2022
	KU_NLP	-	A pipeline system that predicts the mentions and resolves the coreference separately.	Span classification	CODI-CRAC 2022	CODI-CRAC 2022
	DFKI-INRIA	Xu and Choi (2020), Anikina et al. (2021)	The Xu and Choi (2020) was used as the main system for coreference and the output is supplemented with singletons from the Anikina et al. (2021) system	SpaCy	CODI-CRAC 2022 + OntoNotes	CODI-CRAC 2022
Bridging Resolution	UTD_NLP	Yu and Poesio (2020)	Build upon the baseline with SpanBERT as the backbone. Additional dialogue-specific features were used.	Adapted from Xu and Choi (2020)	CODI-CRAC 2022	CODI-CRAC 2022
	DFKI-INRIA	Joshi et al. (2019)	Remove the coarse-to-fine score of the baseline and resolve the bridging in the Gold A setting.	Joshi et al. (2019)	CODI-CRAC 2022 + BASHI + IS-Notes	CODI-CRAC 2022
Discourse Deixis Resolution	UTD_NLP	Xu and Choi (2020)	Using heuristic and a binary classifier to select candidate anaphors. For each selected anaphor up to 10 previous utterances were used as candidate antecedents. Then the system assigns antecedents to each of the candidate anaphors	Obtained as part of joint mention detection and deixis resolution	CODI-CRAC 2022	CODI-CRAC 2022
	DFKI-INRIA	Xu and Choi (2020)	A multi-task learning system learning on both coreference and discourse deixis. With additional anaphor type classifier to filter non-discourse deixis anaphors.	Heuristic for anaphors; antecedents were predicted by the baseline	CODI-CRAC 2022	CODI-CRAC 2022

Table 2: Summary of the Participating Systems

Team	LIGHT	AMI	PERS.	SWBD.	Avg.
		Eval AR			
UTD_NLP	**82.23**	**62.90**	**79.20**	**75.81**	**75.04**
DFKI-INRIA	72.06	51.41	69.87	60.61	63.49
KU_NLP	68.27	48.87	69.06	60.99	61.80
Baseline	54.23	34.14	53.16	49.30	47.71

Table 3: Performance on Task 1 (Evaluation Phase) – Identity Anaphora (CoNLL Avg. F1)

Team	LIGHT	AMI	PERS.	SWBD.	Avg.
		Eval Br (Gold A)			
UTD_NLP	**46.80**	**39.35**	**56.91**	**44.40**	**46.87**
DFKI-INRIA	37.68	35.23	50.99	35.78	39.92
Baseline	29.93	22.69	37.83	30.39	30.21
		Eval Br (Gold M)			
UTD_NLP	**26.77**	**19.65**	**34.59**	**22.74**	**25.94**
Baseline	4.99	8.77	11.49	7.08	8.08
		Eval Br (Pred)			
UTD_NLP	**23.25**	**13.42**	**27.75**	**19.72**	**21.04**
Baseline	4.01	4.66	8.45	4.00	5.28

Table 4: Performance on Task 2 (Evaluation Phase) – Bridging Anaphora (Entity F1)

25% for all four sub-corpora. For LIGHT and PERSUASION, the system achieved CoNLL Avg. F1 scores of 80% or more, the result on the SWITCHBOARD followed closely with an F1 of 76%. The system performance on the toughest sub-corpus (AMI) is way below the other sub-corpora a large 20% gap between LIGHT and AMI are visible across all the participant system as well as the baseline. The reason leads to the large gaps in performance between AMI and other sub-corpora is mainly due to the conversations in AMI being substantially longer than the other corpora. This challenged the systems with a much longer distance between the anaphors and their antecedents.

8.2 Task 2 – Bridging Anaphora

Two teams submitted their results to Task 2, with UTD_NLP participating in all three phases and DFKI-INRIA only participating in the antecedent selection (Gold A) setting. The entity F1 scores for each sub-corpora together with the macro-average of those scores, the latter was used for ranking the systems.

Two teams submitted a total of 102 runs to the leaderboard for three different settings (67 runs for Pred, 5 runs for Gold M and 30 runs for Gold A).

Team	LIGHT	AMI	PERS.	SWBD.	Avg.
		Eval DD (Gold A)			
UTD_NLP	**52.40**	**72.50**	**69.61**	**72.11**	**66.66**
DFKI-INRIA	44.95	56.54	62.79	0.00	41.07
Baseline	40.07	39.89	51.43	37.72	42.28
		Eval DD (Gold M)			
UTD_NLP	**38.38**	**55.12**	**54.89**	**49.83**	**49.56**
DFKI-INRIA	35.91	47.13	48.24	0.00	32.82
Baseline	18.14	22.95	30.15	21.37	23.15
		Eval DD (Pred)			
UTD_NLP	**37.09**	**53.31**	**54.59**	**49.76**	**48.69**
DFKI-INRIA	36.82	50.09	47.04	0.00	33.49
Baseline	10.94	17.39	16.61	13.30	14.56

Table 5: Performance on Task 3 (Evaluation Phase) – Discourse Deixis (CoNLL Avg. F1)

This makes bridging (Task 2) overtaking the identity resolution (Task 1) becomes the most popular task of this year's shared task in terms number of runs submitted to the leaderboard. Table 4 introduces the results of each phases. For the predicted mention setting (Pred), where the systems need to predict both the mentions and the bridging relations, the baseline only achieved a score of 5% on average. The task is very challenging given that only a limited amount of training data is available and the complexity of the bridging task itself. Yet the best result from UTD_NLP quadrupled the ones of the baseline. With the help of available gold mention (Gold M), both the baseline and the UTD_NLP performance further improved slightly by 3-5%. The small improvements achieved by using the gold mentions indicate that 1. the mentions predicted by the systems are not substantially different from the gold mentions; 2. the bridging task remains very challenging even though the gold mentions are provided. In the gold anaphor setting (Gold A) where the gold bridging anaphors are made available in addition to the gold mentions, the system performance increased dramatically. The baseline performance is more than tripled and the best results are 20% higher than the ones of the gold mention (Gold M) setting. Over the four sub-corpora, the PERSUASION seems to be the easiest corpus, both baseline and the participating systems achieved the best results on this corpus. The system results on the other three sub-corpus vary from system to system, in general, no clear distinction between them.

8.3 Task 3 – Discourse Deixis

For Task 3, two teams (UTD_NLP and DFKI-INRIA) participated in all three phases. In total, we received 72 runs from them, in which 30 runs were submitted to the predicted mention setting (Pred), 34 runs for the gold mention setting (Gold M) and 8 runs for the gold anaphor setting (Gold A). The UTD_NLP team submitted results for all four sub-corpora whereas the DFKI-INRIA team submitted predictions for three sub-corpora leaving the SWITCHBOARD behind. We report the CoNLL average F1 for each sub-corpora and rank the systems using the mean of those scores (see Table 5).

For the predicted mention setting, the baseline system achieved a score of around 15% for all four sub-corpora, both participating systems achieved much better results than the baseline. The performances are relatively close for LIGHT and AMI, and for PERSUASION, the UTD_NLP is 7% better than the DFKI-INRIA team. The best performing system achieved CoNLL average F1 scores on or above 50% for all sub-corpora evaluated, the only exception is the LIGHT which is more than 10% lower than other corpora. In the gold mention setting (Gold M), the baseline does improve largely (9%) by further filtering the heuristic anaphors with the gold mentions. However, the additionally available gold mentions do not improve largely the performance of the participating systems. The performance of the DFKI-INRIA team on LIGHT and AMI even dropped slightly. Finally, in the gold anaphor setting (Gold A), the naive baseline already achieved a score above 40%, and the best participating system achieved an F1 above 66% on average. This suggests the identification of discourse deixis anaphor remains challenging. Overall, all the systems outperform the baseline by a large margin in all the sub-corpora they participated.

8.4 Discussion

Since this is the second year of the shared task, we adopted many valuable assets from the first year, such as the scorer, the code to set up the CodaLab and the baselines etc. For this year, one of the main focus becomes to improve the quality of the annotation. We managed to release the revised version of the RST portion of the ARRAU 3 data that serves as the main training data for the shared task. In addition, we also annotated brand new test sets for all sub-corpora and revised the dev/test sets from last year to make them train/dev sets respectively. The consistency of the annotation has been largely improved for this year's shared task data and this makes the corpus of higher quality. We also managed to release most of the data as scheduled. Apart from the data, we also introduced the gold anaphor settings for bridging and discourse deixis tasks to allow the participants to develop systems focused on the antecedent selection subtask. To adapt to the new phase, we extended the baselines from last year to the gold settings.

In terms of the results, although the test sets are not the same as last year, the baseline performance remains similar is a good indication that the hardness of the tasks does not change much. In comparison with last year, we noticed some improvements for both bridging and discourse deixis tasks. The performance on the bridging task improved 3-5% on average and for discourse deixis, we saw large improvements of 6% and 10% for the gold/predicted mention settings respectively. Apart from more advanced systems being used, the additional in-domain training set available this year might also play a role in the improvements. By contrast, the best performances on identity resolution are similar to last year's. This might as a result of the development set that was already used for training by the best-performing system from last year. Hence the settings are not that different between the two years.

Finally, we would like to thank all participants for making a great effort to push further the performances on all the individual tasks. And congratulate them for outperforming the baselines by large margins.

9 Conclusion and Future Work

In this paper we presented a general overview of the CODI-CRAC 2022 shared task. Like the first shared task in this series, CODI-CRAC 2022 focused on resolving three types of anaphoric relations in dialogues: identity, bridging reference, and discourse deixis.

Based on the feedback from participants to the first task, in this second event we released the annotation guidelines beforehand so that participants could know exactly how the data had been annotated. In addition, we re-checked the data newly annotated for the first edition (now available for training and development, so that participants could do some in-domain training as well), and using a larger group of annotators, which resulted in an hopefully more objective annotation. New test data in the four new dialogue domains was also annotated.

The participant systems outperformed the baselines on virtually all tasks and settings, although a clear difference in performance could be observed for bridging reference between pure resolution and resolution + identification. (Interestingly, we didn't observe much difference in performance between the 'Gold Mention' and 'Predicted' settings for either bridging nor discourse deixis.) A clear difference was observed between the results on the AMI datasets and on the other datasets for identity anaphora and bridging reference, possibly due to greater length of the documents in AMI.

Acknowledgments

We are very grateful to Maris Camilleri, Paloma Carretero Garcia, Taiqi He and Katherine Zhang not only for the annotation but for their extensive analysis of the annotation scheme and the data, resulting in useful discussions. We would also like to thank the Linguistic Data Consortium, who very generously made the ARRAU and SWITCHBOARD data available to the participants to the competition.

The work of Massimo Poesio, Juntao Yu, Maris Camilleri and Paloma Carretero Garcia was funded in part by the the DALI project, ERC Grant 695662; in part by the EPSRC project ARCIDUCA, grant number EP/W001632/1; and in part by HITS Heidelberg. The work of Lori Levin, Taiqi He and Katherine Zhang was funded by the Language Technologies Institute at Carnegie Mellon University.

References

Tatiana Anikina, Cennet Oguz, Natalia Skachkova, Siyu Tao, Sharmila Upadhyaya, and Ivana Kruijff-Korbayova. 2021. Anaphora resolution in dialogue: Description of the DFKI-TalkingRobots system for the CODI-CRAC 2021 shared-task. In *Proceedings of the CODI-CRAC 2021 Shared Task on Anaphora, Bridging, and Discourse Deixis in Dialogue*, pages 32–42, Punta Cana, Dominican Republic. Association for Computational Linguistics.

David Bamman, Olivia Lewke, and Anya Mansoor. 2020. An annotated dataset of coreference in english literature. In *Proc. of LREC*. European Language Resources Association (ELRA), Association for Computational Linguistics (ACL).

Donna Byron. 2002. Resolving pronominal references to abstract entities. In *Proc. of the ACL*, pages 80–87.

Jean Carletta. 2006. Announcing the AMI meeting corpus. *The ELRA Newsletter*, 11(1):3–5.

Wallace L. Chafe. 1980. *The Pear Stories: Cognitive, Cultural and Linguistic Aspects of Narrative Production*. Ablex, Norwood, NJ.

Herbert H. Clark. 1977. Bridging. In P. N. Johnson-Laird and P.C. Wason, editors, *Thinking: Readings in Cognitive Science*, pages 411–420. Cambridge University Press, London and New York.

Herbert H. Clark and Susan E. Brennan. 1990. Grounding in communication. In L. B. Resnick, J. Levine, and S. D. Behrend, editors, *Perspectives on Socially Shared Cognition*. APA.

Kevin Bretonnel Cohen, Arrick Lanfranchi, Miji Joo-young Choi, Michael Bada, William A. Baumgartner Jr., Natalya Panteleyeva, Karin Verspoor, Martha Palmer, and Lawrence E. Hunter. 2017. Coreference annotation and resolution in the Colorado Richly Annotated Full Text (CRAFT) corpus of biomedical journal articles. *BMC Bioinformatics*, 18(372).

Miriam Eckert and Michael Strube. 2001. Dialogue acts, synchronising units and anaphora resolution. *Journal of Semantics*.

Carola Eschenbach, Christopher Habel, Michael Herweg, and Klaus Rehkämper. 1989. Remarks on plural anaphora. In *Proceedings of the fourth conference on European chapter of the Association for Computational Linguistics*, pages 161–167. Association for Computational Linguistics.

John J. Godfrey, Edward C. Holliman, and Jane McDaniel. 1992. Switchboard: telephone speech corpus for research and development . acoustics,. In *IEEE International Conference on Speech, and Signal Processing, ICASSP-92*, volume 1, pages 517–520.

Loïc Grobol. 2020. *Coreference resolution for spoken French*. Ph.D. thesis, Université Sorbonne Nouvelle.

John A. Hawkins. 1978. *Definiteness and Indefiniteness*. Croom Helm, London.

Peter A. Heeman and Graeme Hirst. 1995. Collaborating on referring expressions. *Computational Linguistics*, 21(3):351–382.

Yufang Hou. 2020. Bridging anaphora resolution as question answering. In *Proceedings of the 58th Annual Meeting of the Association for Computational Linguistics*, pages 1428–1438, Online. Association for Computational Linguistics.

Yufang Hou, Katja Markert, and Michael Strube. 2018. Unrestricted bridging resolution. *Computational Linguistics*, 44(2):237–284.

Mandar Joshi, Danqi Chen, Yinhan Liu, Daniel S Weld, Luke Zettlemoyer, and Omer Levy. 2020. Spanbert: Improving pre-training by representing and predicting spans. *Transactions of the Association for Computational Linguistics*, 8:64–77.

Mandar Joshi, Omer Levy, Luke Zettlemoyer, and Daniel Weld. 2019. BERT for coreference resolution: Baselines and analysis. In *Proceedings of the 2019 Conference on Empirical Methods in Natural Language Processing and the 9th International Joint Conference on Natural Language Processing (EMNLP-IJCNLP)*, pages 5803–5808, Hong Kong, China. Association for Computational Linguistics.

Hans Kamp and Uwe Reyle. 1993. *From Discourse to Logic*. D. Reidel, Dordrecht.

Ben Kantor and Amir Globerson. 2019. Coreference resolution with entity equalization. In *Proceedings of the 57th Annual Meeting of the Association for Computational Linguistics*, pages 673–677, Florence, Italy. Association for Computational Linguistics.

Sopan Khosla, Juntao Yu, Ramesh Manuvinakurike, Vincent Ng, Massimo Poesio, Michael Strube, and Carolyn Rosé. 2021. The CODI-CRAC 2021 shared task on anaphora, bridging, and discourse deixis in dialogue. In *Proceedings of the CODI-CRAC 2021 Shared Task on Anaphora, Bridging, and Discourse Deixis in Dialogue*, pages 1–15, Punta Cana, Dominican Republic. Association for Computational Linguistics.

Hideo Kobayashi, Shengjie Li, and Vincent Ng. 2021. Neural anaphora resolution in dialogue. In *Proceedings of the CODI-CRAC 2021 Shared Task on Anaphora, Bridging, and Discourse Deixis in Dialogue*, pages 16–31, Punta Cana, Dominican Republic. Association for Computational Linguistics.

Hideo Kobayashi and Vincent Ng. 2021. Bridging resolution: Making sense of the state of the art. In *Proceedings of the 2021 Conference of the North American Chapter of the Association for Computational Linguistics: Human Language Technologies*, pages 1652–1659, Online. Association for Computational Linguistics.

Varada Kolhatkar, Adam Roussel, Stefanie Dipper, and Heike Zinsmeister. 2018. Anaphora with non-nominal antecedents in computational linguistics: a Survey. *Computational Linguistics*, 44(3):547–612.

Kenton Lee, Luheng He, Mike Lewis, and Luke Zettlemoyer. 2017. End-to-end neural coreference resolution. In *Proceedings of the 2017 Conference on Empirical Methods in Natural Language Processing*, pages 188–197, Copenhagen, Denmark. Association for Computational Linguistics.

Kenton Lee, Luheng He, and Luke Zettlemoyer. 2018. Higher-order coreference resolution with coarse-to-fine inference. In *Proceedings of the 2018 Conference of the North American Chapter of the Association for Computational Linguistics: Human Language Technologies, Volume 2 (Short Papers)*, pages 687–692.

Quan Liu, Hui Jiang, Andrew Evdokimov, Zhen-Hua Ling, Xiaodan Zhu, Si Wei, and Yu Hu. 2017. Cause-effect knowledge acquisition and neural association model for solving a set of winograd schema problems. In *Proceedings of the Twenty-Sixth International Joint Conference on Artificial Intelligence, IJCAI-17*, pages 2344–2350.

Pengcheng Lu and Massimo Poesio. 2021. Coreference resolution for the biomedical domain: A survey. In *Proc. of the CRAC Workshop*.

Ana Marasović, Leo Born, Juri Opitz, and Anette Frank. 2017. A mention-ranking model for abstract anaphora resolution. In *Proceedings of the 2017 Conference on Empirical Methods in Natural Language Processing*, pages 221–232, Copenhagen, Denmark. Association for Computational Linguistics.

Mitchell P. Marcus, Beatrice Santorini, and Mary Ann Marcinkiewicz. 1993. Building a large annotated corpus of english: the Penn Treebank. *Computational Linguistics*, 19(2):313–330.

Katja Markert, Yufang Hou, and Michael Strube. 2012. Collective classification for fine-grained information status. In *Proc. of the ACL*, Juju island, Korea.

Mark-Christoph Müller. 2008. *Fully Automatic Resolution of It, This And That in Unrestricted Multy-Party Dialog*. Ph.D. thesis, Universität Tübingen.

Mark-Christoph Müller and Michael Strube. 2006. Multi-level annotation of linguistic data with mmax2. In S. Braun, K. Kohn, and J. Mukherjee, editors, *Corpus Technology and Language Pedagogy. New Resources, New Tools, New Methods*, volume 3 of *English Corpus Linguistics*, pages 197–214. Peter Lang.

Judith Muzerelle, Anaïs Lefeuvre, Emmanuel Schang, Jean-Yves Antoine, Aurore Pelletier, Denis Maurel, Iris Eshkol, and Jeanne Villaneau. 2014. Ancor_centre, a large free spoken french coreference corpus. In *Proc. of LREC*.

Anna Nedoluzhko. 2013. Generic noun phrases and annotation of coreference and bridging relations in the prague dependency treebank. In *Proc. of LAW*, pages 103–111.

Anna Nedoluzhko, Michal Novák, Martin Popel, Zdeněk Žabokrtský, and Daniel Zeman. 2021. Coreference meets universal dependencies – a pilot experiment on harmonizing coreference datasets for 11 languages. ÚFAL Technical Report TR-2021-66, Charles University, Prague.

Malvina Nissim, Shipra Dingare, Jean Carletta, and Mark Steedman. 2004. An annotation scheme for information status in dialogue. In *Proc. of LREC*.

Silviu Paun, Juntao Yu, Nafise Sadat Moosavi, and Massimo Poesio. 2022. Scoring coreference chains with split-antecedent anaphors.

Massimo Poesio. 2004. Discourse annotation and semantic annotation in the GNOME corpus. In *Proc. of the ACL Workshop on Discourse Annotation*, pages 72–79, Barcelona.

Massimo Poesio and Ron Artstein. 2008. Anaphoric annotation in the ARRAU corpus. In *Proc. of LREC*, Marrakesh.

Massimo Poesio, Jon Chamberlain, Udo Kruschwitz, Silviu Paun, Alexandra Uma, and Juntao Yu. 2019. A crowdsourced corpus of multiple judgments and disagreement on anaphoric interpretation. In *Proc. of NAACL*, page 1778–1789, Minneapolis. Association for Computational Linguistics (ACL).

Massimo Poesio, Yulia Grishina, Varada Kolhatkar, Nafise Moosavi, Ina Roesiger, Adam Roussel, Fabian Simonjetz, Alexandra Uma, Olga Uryupina, Juntao Yu, and Heike Zinsmeister. 2018. Anaphora resolution with the ARRAU corpus. In *Proceedings of the First Workshop on Computational Models of Reference, Anaphora and Coreference*, pages 11–22, New Orleans, Louisiana. Association for Computational Linguistics.

Massimo Poesio, Sameer Pradhan, Marta Recasens, Kepa Rodriguez, and Yannick Versley. 2016. Annotated corpora and annotation tools. In M. Poesio, R. Stuckardt, and Y. Versley, editors, *Anaphora Resolution: Algorithms, Resources and Applications*, chapter 4. Springer.

Massimo Poesio and Hannes Rieser. 2010. Completions, coordination, and alignment in dialogue. *Dialogue and Discourse*, 1(1):1–89.

Sameer Pradhan, Alessandro Moschitti, Nianwen Xue, Olga Uryupina, and Yuchen Zhang. 2012. CoNLL-2012 shared task: Modeling multilingual unrestricted coreference in OntoNotes. In *Proceedings of the Sixteenth Conference on Computational Natural Language Learning (CoNLL 2012)*, Jeju, Korea.

Ellen F. Prince. 1981. Toward a taxonomy of given-new information. In P. Cole, editor, *Radical Pragmatics*, pages 223–256. Academic Press, New York.

Altaf Rahman and Vincent Ng. 2012. Resolving complex cases of definite pronouns: The Winograd schema challenge. In *Proceedings of the 2012 Joint Conference on Empirical Methods in Natural Language Processing and Computational Natural Language Learning*, pages 777–789, Jeju Island, Korea. Association for Computational Linguistics.

Marta Recasens and M. Antònia Martí. 2010. AnCora-CO: Coreferentially annotated corpora for Spanish and Catalan. *Language Resources and Evaluation*, 44(4):315–345.

Keisuke Sakaguchi, Ronan Le Bras, Chandra Bhagavatula, and Yejin Choi. 2020. Winogrande: An adversarial winograd schema challenge at scale. *Proceedings of the AAAI Conference on Artificial Intelligence*, 34:8732–8740.

Andreas Stolcke, Klaus Ries, Noah Coccaro, Elizabeth Shriberg, Rebecca Bates, Daniel Jurafsky, Paul Taylor, Rachel Martin, Carol Van-Ess-Dykema, and Marie Meteer. 1997. Dialogue act modeling for automatic tagging and recognition of conversational speech. *Computational Linguistics*, 26(3):339–371.

Jack Urbanek, Angela Fan, Siddharth Karamcheti, Saachi Jain, Emily Dinan, Tim Rocktäschel, Douwe Kiela, Arthur Szlam, Samuel Humeau, and Jason Weston. 2019. Learning to speak and act in a fantasy text adventure game. ArXiv preprint arXiv:1903.03094.

Olga Uryupina, Ron Artstein, Antonella Bristot, Federica Cavicchio, Francesca Delogu, Kepa J. Rodriguez, and Massimo Poesio. 2020. Annotating a broad range of anaphoric phenomena, in a variety of genres: the ARRAU corpus. *Journal of Natural Language Engineering*.

Hardik Vala, Andrew Piper, and Derek Ruths. 2016. The more antecedents, the merrier: Resolving multi-antecedent anaphors. In *Proceedings of the 54th Annual Meeting of the Association for Computational Linguistics (Volume 1: Long Papers)*, pages 2287–2296, Berlin, Germany. Association for Computational Linguistics.

Yannick Versley. 2008. Vagueness and referential ambiguity in a large-scale annotated corpus. *Research on Language and Computation*, 6:333–353.

Xuewei Wang, Weiyan Shi, Richard Kim, Yoojung Oh, Sijia Yang, Jingwen Zhang, and Zhou Yu. 2019. Persuasion for good: Towards a personalized persuasive dialogue system for social good. In *Proc. of ACL*.

Bonnie L. Webber. 1991. Structure and ostension in the interpretation of discourse deixis. *Language and Cognitive Processes*, 6(2):107–135.

Kellie Webster, Marta Recasens, Vera Axelrod, and Jason Baldridge. 2018. Mind the GAP: A balanced corpus of gendered ambiguous pronouns. *Transactions of the Association for Computational Linguistics*, 6:605–617.

Sam Wiseman, Alexander M. Rush, Stuart Shieber, and Jason Weston. 2015. Learning anaphoricity and antecedent ranking features for coreference resolution. In *Proceedings of the 53rd Annual Meeting of the Association for Computational Linguistics and the 7th International Joint Conference on Natural Language Processing (Volume 1: Long Papers)*, pages 1416–1426, Beijing, China. Association for Computational Linguistics.

Liyan Xu and Jinho D Choi. 2020. Revealing the myth of higher-order inference in coreference resolution. In *Proceedings of the 2020 Conference on Empirical*

Methods in Natural Language Processing (EMNLP), pages 8527–8533.

Juntao Yu, Bernd Bohnet, and Massimo Poesio. 2020a. Neural mention detection. In *Proceedings of the 12th Conference on Language Resources and Evaluation (LREC 2020)*.

Juntao Yu, Sopan Khosla, Nafise Sadat Moosavi, Silviu Paun, Sameer Pradhan, and Massimo Poesio. 2022. The universal anaphora scorer. In *Proceedings of the Language Resources and Evaluation Conference*, pages 4873–4883, Marseille, France. European Language Resources Association.

Juntao Yu, Nafise Sadat Moosavi, Silviu Paun, and Massimo Poesio. 2020b. Free the plural: Unrestricted split-antecedent anaphora resolution. In *Proceedings of the 28th International Conference on Computational Linguistics*, pages 6113–6125, Barcelona, Spain (Online). International Committee on Computational Linguistics.

Juntao Yu, Nafise Sadat Moosavi, Silviu Paun, and Massimo Poesio. 2021. Stay together: A system for single and split-antecedent anaphora resolution. In *Proceedings of the 2021 Conference of the North American Chapter of the Association for Computational Linguistics: Human Language Technologies*. Association for Computational Linguistics.

Juntao Yu and Massimo Poesio. 2020. Multitask learning based neural bridging reference resolution. In *Proceedings of the 28th International Conference on Computational Linguistics*, pages 3534–3546, Barcelona, Spain (Online). International Committee on Computational Linguistics.

Amir Zeldes. 2017. The GUM corpus: Creating multilayer resources in the classroom. *Language Resources and Evaluation*, 51(3):581–612.

Ethan Zhou and Jinho D. Choi. 2018. They exist! introducing plural mentions to coreference resolution and entity linking. In *Proceedings of the 27th International Conference on Computational Linguistics*, pages 24–34, Santa Fe, New Mexico, USA. Association for Computational Linguistics.

Yilun Zhu, Sameer Pradhan, and Amir Zeldes. 2021. OntoGUM: Evaluating contextualized SOTA coreference resolution on 12 more genres. In *Proceedings of the 59th Annual Meeting of the Association for Computational Linguistics and the 11th International Joint Conference on Natural Language Processing (Volume 2: Short Papers)*, pages 461–467, Online. Association for Computational Linguistics.

Anaphora Resolution in Dialogue: System Description (CODI-CRAC 2022 Shared Task)

Tatiana Anikina
Natalia Skachkova
DFKI / Saarland Informatics Campus,
Saarbrücken, Germany
tatiana.anikina@dfki.de
natalia.skachkova@dfki.de

Joseph Renner
Priyansh Trivedi
Inria,
Nancy, France
joseph.renner@inria.fr
priyansh.trivedi@inria.fr

Abstract

We describe three models submitted for the CODI-CRAC 2022 shared task. To perform identity anaphora resolution, we test several combinations of the incremental clustering approach based on the Workspace Coreference System (WCS) with other coreference models. The best result is achieved by adding the "cluster merging" version of the *coref-hoi* model, which brings up to 10.33% improvement[1] over vanilla WCS clustering. Discourse deixis resolution is implemented as multi-task learning: we combine the learning objective of *coref-hoi* with anaphor type classification. We adapt the higher-order resolution model introduced in Joshi et al. (2019) for bridging resolution given gold mentions and anaphors.

1 Introduction

In this paper we present our systems submitted for the CODI-CRAC 2022 Shared Task (CCST) on Anaphora, Bridging, and Discourse Deixis in Dialogue[2] (Yu et al., 2022). The task is a follow-up to the one held last year and described in Khosla et al. (2021). As its name suggests, besides identity anaphora this shared task tries to cover other, less-studied, anaphoric phenomena, and offers new multi-genre data that combines several types of annotations in Universal Anaphora[3] format.

Main focus of the shared task is on dialogue. Dialogue data offers new challenges, like grammatically incorrect utterances, disfluencies, more deictic references, speaker grounding and long-distance conversation structure (Khosla et al., 2021). While coreference resolution in text has been very actively studied in the recent years, it is much less researched in dialogue, especially such forms as bridging, or discourse deixis. Descriptions of early systems implemented for the resolution of 'standard' and discourse deictic pronouns in dialogue can be found, e.g., in Byron (2002), Strube and Müller (2003), Müller (2008). More approaches (not implemented), together with some useful findings are presented, e.g., in Rocha (1999), Eckert and Strube (2000), and Navarretta (2004).

CCST 2021 stirred new interest in coreference resolution in dialogue. The majority of systems submitted for it represent various modifications of either the higher-order coreference resolution model (*coref-hoi*) by Xu and Choi (2020), or one of the earlier models by Joshi et al. (2019) and Lee et al. (2018). These models were originally trained on the text data, and are span-based - each span gets associated with a score, and anaphor-antecedent pairs are established based on the pairwise scores. Designed for identity anaphora resolution, these models were also adapted for bridging and discourse deixis resolution. Examples of span-based models submitted for CCST 2021 include systems by Kobayashi et al. (2021), Renner et al. (2021), Xu and Choi (2021). Other participants presented different approaches. Thus, Kim et al. (2021) perform identity anaphora and bridging resolution using pointer networks. Anikina et al. (2021) cast anaphora resolution as a clustering problem, and discourse deixis resolution - as a Siamese Net based scoring function.

Inspired by the success of the span-based coreference resolution models, we submit three independent systems for CCST 2022. Our system for identity anaphora resolution uses both the Workspace Coreference System by Anikina et al. (2021) and the *coref-hoi* model as described in Section 2. The model for discourse deixis extends *coref-hoi* with shallow linguistic features and aims at resolving three types of potential anaphors. It is described in Section 3. The model for bridging resolution is a modification of the system by Renner et al. (2021). The approach is explained in Section 4.

[1] An average improvement over all 4 datasets is 7.95%.
[2] https://codalab.lisn.upsaclay.fr/competitions/614#learn_the_details
[3] https://universalanaphora.github.io/UniversalAnaphora/

Proceedings of the CODI-CRAC 2022 Shared Task on Anaphora, Bridging, and Discourse Deixis in Dialogue, pages 15–27
Gyeongju, Republic of Korea, October 17, 2022.
https://doi.org/10.26615/978-954-452-056-4_002

2 Anaphora Resolution

For the anaphora resolution track we trained and combined the outputs of the Workspace Coreference System (WCS) and the *coref-hoi* system (see Table 1). While working on the shared task we realized that a combination of different models performs better than a single model and we explored various settings to find an optimal solution.

2.1 Data

For training of the WCS system we used the datasets recommended by the shared task organizers. These include the ARRAU corpus (Gnome, Trains_91, Trains_93, RST_DTreeBank, Pear_stories), AMI, Switchboard, Light and Persuasion data. We used the development sets of AMI, Light and Persuasion for the internal evaluation and comparison of different configurations. We trained our system using the gold mention spans to avoid any mistakes introduced by the mention extraction module and used SpaCy (Honnibal et al., 2020) for mention extraction during the test phase.

For training of the *coref-hoi* system, we utilized the CoNLL 2012 English Shared Task dataset (Pradhan et al., 2012) to supplement the datasets listed in the previous paragraph. Note that this CoNLL 2012 data does not include singleton coreference clusters, but the current dialogue shared task datasets do.

2.2 Model architecture

WCS Our model is based on the implementation described in Anikina et al. (2021). It creates coreference clusters incrementally and compares each new mention to the clusters that are available in the workspace. The general flow of the model is presented in Figure 1. The model uses separate layers to encode each pair of mentions where one mention represents a workspace cluster and another mention is a candidate that is being clustered. WCS passes the concatenated embeddings of the candidate mention and the cluster member through several feed-forward neural layers with the input and output dimensions shown in Table 2.

The network also encodes the absolute position of each mention within the document and generates a separate embedding for each speaker. The model combines this information with different word embeddings. For each mention it extracts the head and encodes it with a combination of contextual BERT embeddings (Devlin et al., 2018) (`bert-base-cased`) together with GloVe (Pennington et al., 2014) and Numberbatch (Speer et al., 2017) embeddings. Unlike Anikina et al. (2021) we do not generate a new random embedding for each unknown word, but take an average embedding based on all words in the GloVe and Numberbatch vocabularies. This gave us slightly better results in the pilot experiments.

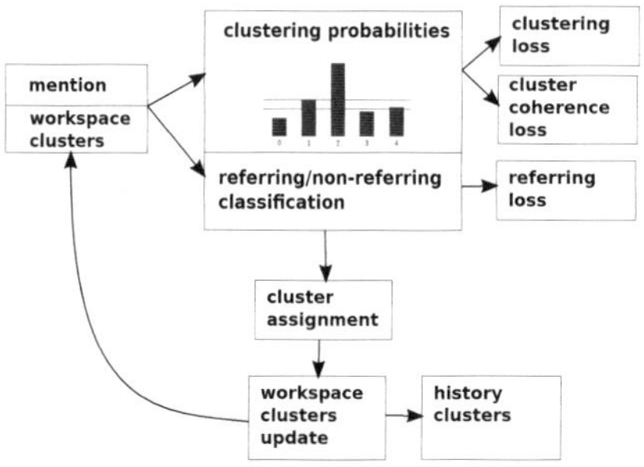

Figure 1: Workspace Coreference System Overview

In order to represent the spans we take an average of all individual word embeddings based on BERT and GloVe correspondingly. We also experimented with SpanBERT embeddings but did not observe any improvements. E.g., when we replaced our span embeddings with SpanBERT and left the rest of the system unchanged we achieved 66.68% CoNLL F1 score when training and evaluating on the Light dataset. After replacing SpanBERT with standard BERT and simply averaging span embeddings we achieved 67.23% CoNLL F1 score on the same data. Removing GloVe embeddings and leaving only BERT, SpanBERT and Numberbatch or training on more data samples also did not help. We suspect that since SpanBERT embeddings have high dimensionality (representing span start, span end and span head) they dominate mention representation in WCS and allow some vague semantic matches. E.g., with SpanBERT we generated clusters that included mentions like *'war'* and *'peace'* or *'the jamaica tourist board'* and *'jamaican'*. Training for more epochs or adjusting hyperparameters might help to improve clustering but the configurations that we tested have not shown an improvement.

The WCS system combines three cross-entropy losses that are added in each forward pass. The main clustering loss compares the true cluster probabilities vs. the computed ones. The true probabilities are computed with respect to the mentions that are currently in the workspace. For each mention

Track	Resolution of anaphoric identities
Setting	Predicted mentions
Baseline	WCS (Anikina et al., 2021) and *coref-hoi* model (Xu and Choi, 2020)
Approach	1) Extract all nominal phrases with SpaCy 2) Run WCS trained on the Shared Task dialogue data 3) Run *coref-hoi* with cluster merging trained on the CoNLL 2012 data 4) Combine the outputs of WCS and *coref-hoi*
Train data	ARRAU corpus (Gnome, Trains_91, Trains_93, RST_DTreeBank, Pear_stories), AMI, Switchboard, Light and Pesuasion, CoNLL 2012 English dataset
Dev data	AMI, Light, Persuasion, ARRAU (dev splits)

Table 1: Anaphora resolution: approach summary

Encoder	Input dim	Hidden dim	Output dim
BERT head	2*768	900	600
BERT span	2*768	900	600
Numberbatch	2*300	600	300
GloVe head	2*100	600	200
GloVe span	2*100	600	200
BERT masked LM	2*768	600	200

Table 2: Separate encoders are used to represent mention pairs in WCS. Additionally, distance between the mentions, their positions in the document and corresponding speakers are encoded and added to the final representation.

the probability of being in that cluster is defined as the ratio of mentions that are in the same gold cluster and the current cluster over all mentions in that cluster. The coherence loss computes the difference between the gold cluster assignments and the system assignments. Basically, we create two matrices that align mentions to each other and check the overlap between these matrices in the gold annotations vs. the generated outputs (the matrix has ones if two mentions belong to the same cluster and zeros otherwise). The referring loss is used for the referring expression classification which is a binary classification task. It is needed since not all mention spans extracted by SpaCy are valid referring expressions.

After computing clustering probabilities for each mention and clusters in the workspace we apply softmax and select the cluster with the highest probability. After that the workspace is updated and some clusters are moved to the history if they have not been updated for more than 100 steps. After the initial clustering we apply some post-processing as explained in Anikina et al. (2021).

We have also evaluated WCS in combination with a Crosslingual Coreference System (CCS) based on AllenNLP and SpaCy pipelines[4]. We noticed that WCS performs quite well on identifying singletons and clusters with personal pronouns but has more difficulties with other nominal phrases. Hence, in one of the experiments we combined the output of the CCS model trained on OntoNotes that uses MiniLM (Wang et al., 2020) for mention representation with the outputs of WCS trained on the shared task data. Among the clusters generated with CCS we selected only those that do not contain any personal pronouns and from WCS we took singletons and clusters with pronouns.

We also experimented with some compatibility checks. E.g., we checked whether the first and second mentions in the cluster have the same number and we removed the first mention from the WCS cluster if the embedding similarity between the first pronoun and the first noun in that cluster was too low (compared to the cosine similarity between the first pronoun and other mentions in the cluster). E.g., mentions such as *'a presenter'* and *'I'* could belong to the same cluster with pronouns but mentions like *'table'* and *'I'* should not. We run WCS with these modifications on the shared task test set and report our results in Table 3. The final version that was submitted to the leaderboard combines WCS outputs with the *coref-hoi* system as described in the next section.

Coref-HOI Combination We trained a "cluster merging" variant of the *coref-hoi* model. As this model was developed using the data from 2012 CoNLL dataset, which does not include singleton clusters, the model does not output singleton predictions off the shelf (one could potentially use the scores for the "dummy" antecedent as a proxy, but this could be noisy as the model is not trained to differentiate singleton clusters from simple mentions

[4]https://pypi.org/project/crosslingual-coreference/

Setting	Light	AMI	Persuasion	Swbd.
Vanilla WCS	65.96	46.04	59.54	50.63
WCS + CCS	67.27	46.68	63.46	53.92
WCS + CCS + filter	67.46	46.70	63.51	54.07
WCS + coref-hoi	72.06	51.41	69.87	60.61

Table 3: Evaluation of WCS in combination with other coreference systems on the shared task test set. Filter in the third row refers to the incompatibility check

that are not part of any cluster).

Using the development sets of the shared task datasets, we evaluated WCS and the *coref-hoi* model. Results are shown in Table 4. Looking at these scores, we found that *coref-hoi* struggled with singleton clusters (as expected), as the CoNLL F1 score of these predictions was much higher after removing the singletons from the annotations. WCS, on the other hand, seemed to do better on singletons than non-singletons, as evidenced by the higher scores on annotations that contain singletons vs. those without. As a result, we combined the strengths of the two systems by simply adding the singletons predictions of WCS to the cluster predictions of *coref-hoi*. This resulted in the highest test set scores (as shown in Table 3).

2.3 Training

WCS The WCS system was trained for 5 epochs on Nvidia GeForce RTX 2080. We use teacher forcing for the coreference clusters with a ratio of 30%. The learning rate is set to 1e-4 and the dropout rate is 0.3. We use Adam as optimizer. It took about 26 hours to train the whole system on the complete training set.

Coref-HOI The *coref-hoi* system was trained for 24 epochs on a Nvidia Quadro RTX 6000. We use a pretrained $\text{SpanBERT}_{\text{Large}}$ model to initialize the base language model. We use a learning rate of 1e-5 for the base model and 3e-4 for the fine tuning layers. We follow all other hyperparameters found in the *train_spanbert_large_ml0_cm_fn1000* training configuration of the *coref-hoi* system. Training took about 24 hours.

2.4 Results and discussion

Our results on the internal development set as well as on the official test set are reported in Tables 3 and 4. Based on the final cluster assignments we can recognize 4 common types of mistakes made by WCS: partial word overlaps (e.g., *'mute button'* and *'volume button'*), embedded mentions (e.g., *'a power supply which we get'* and *'we'*), wrong span boundaries (e.g., *'ok good knight'*) and confusing candidates that have similar surface forms but different meanings (e.g., *'the minutes of uh this meeting'* and *'forty minutes'*). Some of these mistakes were probably caused by the over-reliance of WCS on the head embeddings. Interestingly, when using SpanBERT instead of GloVe and standard BERT for span encoding we observed that many generated clusters contain mentions with spurious connections (e.g., *'the spirits of our people'* and *'such dark superstitions'* or *'the executive'* and *'the company'*).

Judging from the scores on the development set reported in Table 4, WCS shows better performance than *coref-hoi* when the evaluation is done on all clusters including singletons. However, when singletons are excluded *coref-hoi* outperforms WCS and this was the main motivation to combine the outputs of both models. We also evaluated the span extraction performance of WCS vs. the combined system using the gold mention span annotations provided by the shared task organizers. We found that WCS had consistently higher recall but lower precision on mention span detection compared to the combined model. E.g., on the AMI dataset WCS achieved precision 82% and recall 68% whereas the combined model achieved precision 84% and recall 63%. Similar results were observed on the other two datasets that we tested (Light and Persuasion).

Looking at the mistakes of the combined model we found that some mentions have incorrect spans, e.g., *'half'* and *'hour'* are annotated as two separate mentions in *'see you in half and hour'*. Sometimes the annotated spans are longer than the gold ones, e.g., *'close tabs on you'* instead of *'close tabs'* or *'Of course , good Monk'* instead of *'good Monk'*. This can also result in incorrect clustering such as in case of putting *'this realm'* and *'this realm, stories, population'* in the same cluster. The combined model also struggles with the cases like *'some'* and *'they'* in the following example: ***'Some** don't give the money out like they are suppose to. Did you heard that **they** now do every payment taken from people transparent?'* Both mentions were assigned to the same coreference chain although *'some'* should refer to the people who give the money and *'they'* to those who receive it. Despite some problems with the mention span detection the combined model shows overall better

Setting	Light	Light NS	AMI	AMI NS	Persuasion	Persuasion NS	ARRAU	ARRAU NS
WCS	65.39	61.48	43.33	35.85	61.23	56.55	45.02	32.93
coref-hoi	59.84	76.89	43.30	54.70	60.60	81.00	48.32	66.97

Table 4: Evaluation of WCS and *coref-hoi* on dev sets. NS (No Singletons) refers to annotations with singleton clusters removed. Scores presented are CoNLL F1 scores. Note that the scores are from an internal development set.

clustering performance compared to vanilla WCS.

Experimenting with various combinations of the coreference systems we found that combining the strengths of different systems helps to improve the results. In the future we plan to investigate whether adding coreference signal from the pre-trained models also helps boost the performance and reduce training time for systems like WCS.

For the current submission we combined the model outputs based on some simple heuristics but it would be interesting to see whether this process could be also learned by a model. Training a new model from scratch or even fine-tuning it on a new dataset might be sub-optimal or even not feasible in some cases. E.g., when we deal with dialogues instead of narrative texts or if the annotation schemes differ significantly. In such cases we believe that using a smart coreference editor that combines and checks outputs of different systems and applies some constraints or filters would be beneficial and we would like to work on such project in the future.

3 Discourse Deixis Resolution

CCST 2022 offers three different tracks for discourse deixis resolution. First track (Eval-DD Pred) assumes finding antecedents for discourse deixis anaphors predicted by models given unannotated data. The second one (Eval-DD Gold M) aims at identification of discourse deixis anaphors among all types of annotated anaphors and non-referential mentions, and their subsequent resolution. The goal of the last track (Eval-DD Gold A) is to find antecedents for already annotated discourse deixis anaphors. Our team participated in all three tracks.

The core of our approach relies on the *coref-hoi* model, because it was successfully adopted for CCST 2021 discourse deixis track by Kobayashi et al. (2021). Their model was able to achieve the CoNLL F1 score of 35.4% - 52.1% depending on the dataset and shared task track, and ranked first for discourse deixis (Kobayashi et al., 2021). The summary of our system can be found in Table 5.

3.1 Data

We use training and development data presented in Section 2.1. *Coref-hoi* splits input data into segments of a set length to limit the number of mention candidates. Given a segment, all possible spans/potential mentions are created. Next, this 'pool' of mentions is used to form valid anaphor-antecedent pairs. In contrast to that, we only consider the occurrences of *'this'*, *'that'*, *'it'* and *'which'* as potential anaphors and treat all other spans in the segment as antecedent candidates. These four markables were chosen based on our observation that they often occur as discourse deixis anaphors in our training data: they make about 72.3% of all annotated discourse deictic anaphors[5]. Similar statistical findings (however, for other dialogue corpora) were reported, e.g., by Webber (1988), Müller (2008), Kolhatkar et al. (2018). Besides being discourse deictic, the markables in focus can also be non-referential (e.g., *'it'* in expletive constructions, *'that'* as a relative pronoun), or anaphoric (e.g., *'this'* as a determiner in a noun phrase).

Because we focus only on certain anaphor candidates, we build segments in a slightly different way than *coref-hoi* does. Instead of splitting the input into non-overlapping chunks of approximately the same length, we go through the input data word by word until any of our anaphors occurs, and then create a segment. Our segment typically includes all (sub)tokens up to the current sentence end to the right of the anaphor, as well as one or more sentences to the left of it. We limit the segment's length by 256 (sub)tokens. Thus, given the same input, we build more segments than *coref-hoi* does, our segments are mostly overlapping, and each one contains only one anaphor candidate.

In total we build 9,827 segments/examples from training data, of which 44% contain non-referential *'this'*, *'that'*, *'it'* and *'which'*, 41.2% - anaphoric, and only 14.8% - discourse deictic ones. To make our training data balanced, we perform undersam-

[5]We treat all discourse deictic markables with semantic type 'discourse old' as anaphors.

Track	Resolution of discourse deixis
Setting	Predicted mentions / Gold mentions / Gold anaphors
Baseline	The *coref-hoi* model adopted for discourse deixis by Kobayashi et al. (2021)
Approach	1) Consider all mentions of *this*, *that*, *it* and *which* potential anaphors 2) Consider all spans in the given segment potential antecedents 3) Represent both anaphor and antecedent candidates as embeddings with additional shallow linguistic features 4) Calculate pairwise anaphor-antecedent scores similar to *coref-hoi* and choose the antecedent based on the largest score 5) Use anaphor-antecedent pair representation to classify the anaphor type and discard non-discourse deictic anaphors
Train data	ARRAU corpus (Gnome, Trains_91, Trains_93, RST_DTreeBank, Pear_stories), AMI, Switchboard, Light and Persuasion
Dev data	AMI, Light, Persuasion (dev splits)

Table 5: Discourse deixis resolution: approach summary

pling and decrease the number of examples from the first two classes. We end up having 1,454 training samples of each anaphor class. For the sake of simplicity, undersampling is done blindly, i.e. we do not take into consideration how the instances of our three classes are distributed given each of the four markables.

3.2 Model architecture

We perform discourse deixis resolution using a multi-task learning approach - besides finding the antecedents, we also need to identify the types of potential anaphors (discourse deictic, anaphoric or non-referential). Type classification is performed after the antecedent (if any) is found. It is also important to emphasize that we try to resolve any potential anaphor regardless of its type. Thus, our model also learns to resolve 'standard' coreference as a by-product. To our knowledge, our model is the first one doing that.

To perform the resolution, *coref-hoi* first associates each span (represented as an embedding) with a score indicating how likely this span is a valid mention (anaphor or antecedent). To speed up the training process, certain number of spans with the low scores get pruned. Next, the model learns to find the most probable antecedent for each anaphor based on their pairwise scores.

We modify their approach as follows. First, as we know exactly which span our anaphor x is, and it is the same for all antecedent candidates y, we do not score anaphors or calculate pairwise mention scores. An antecedent score $s_m(y)$ is produced by a feedforward neural network $FFNN_m$ taking as input a vector representation of span y, like in *coref-hoi*. Second, as shown in Table 6, anaphors $k_x = p_x, \rho(x)$ and antecedents $q_y = g_y, \psi(y)$ are composed differently. Main representations p_x and g_y are concatenated with shallow linguistic features $\rho(x)$ and $\psi(y)$ to help our model better differentiate between types of anaphors and antecedent candidates. Our approach to mention representation and motivation behind it are explained in more detail in Section 3.3. Third, we do not prune any unlikely antecedents due to the fact that each segment only contains one anaphor, which often has only one antecedent (if mention is anaphoric, there can be more). If we apply pruning, this only antecedent is very likely to be lost at the early stages of training.

$$\begin{aligned} s(x,y) &= s_m(y) + s_f(x,y) + s_s(x,y) \\ s_m(y) &= FFNN_m(q_y) \\ q_y &= g_y, \psi(y) \\ k_x &= p_x, \rho(x) \\ s_f(x,y) &= k_x \cdot q_y \\ s_s(x,y) &= FFNN_c(k_x, q_y, \phi(x,y)) \end{aligned} \qquad (1)$$

As shown in Equation group 1, the final anaphor-antecedent score is the sum of three components: (1) anaphor score $s_m(y)$; (2) fast score $s_f(x,y)$, which is an inner product of vectors k_x and q_y representing anaphor and antecedent, respectively; (3) slow score $s_s(x,y)$, which is an output of a different network $FFNN_c$ taking as input an anaphor-antecedent pair and pairwise features $\phi(x,y)$. Two of pairwise features are borrowed from the *coref-hoi* model. They are distance feature, showing how many sentences/utterances lie between the starting tokens of two mentions, and similarity feature, which is simply a result of am element-wise multiplication of anaphor and antecedent candidate

$p_x, \rho(x)$	$g_y, \psi(y)$	$\phi(x, y)$
token emb. parent emb. local context emb.	start emb. end emb. weighted avg. emb.	sentence dist. emb. token dist. emb. similarity emb.
POS tag emb. DEP tag emb.	span width emb. span type emb. end token POS emb. end token DEP emb.	

Table 6: Representations of anaphor and antecedent candidates, and pairwise features

vectors. Finally, we add a token distance feature that shows how many (sub)tokens lie between the starting tokens of the two mentions. This feature is used to help our model learn that in case both anaphor and its antecedent are parts of the same sentence, their starting tokens cannot be close to each other.

The largest $s(x, y)$ score is used to predict the best antecedent candidate. The antecedent gets concatenated with the anaphor and is used as input for an anaphor type classifier, which is a multi-layer perceptron (MLP) network consisting of two linear layers with a ReLU activation function in-between. Similar to *coref-hoi,* to account for the case of non-referential 'anaphors', a dummy zero score is always prepended to the row of $s(x, y)$ scores.

3.3 Mention representation

Potential anaphors and antecedents have different representations. While the main part of an antecedent candidate embedding g_y is constructed similar to *coref-hoi*, the main part of an anaphor embedding p_x is a concatenation of the embedding of the token itself, embedding of the parent token and local context embedding, which includes eight (sub)tokens to the left and right of the anaphor.

Our decision to include the last two embeddings was motivated by the following observations. Depending on the mention type, mentions' parents have to certain extent different distributions, e.g., discourse deictic mentions more often have forms of the verb *'to be'* as parents than mentions of other two types (see Table 11 in Appendix A). Moreover, in our data about 60% of anaphor candidates have verbal parents. And certain verbs (e.g., *'assume'*, *'say'*) are only compatible with discourse deixis (Eckert and Strube, 2000). We use SpaCy to identify tokens' parents, and SpanBERT$_{\text{Large}}$ encoder to acquire tokens' embeddings. The usage of context helps capture various useful patterns that may be characteristic of discourse deixis or identity anaphora. These patterns may include, e.g., adjective-copula constructions. Subjects of such constructions with adjectives applicable to abstract entities (e.g., *'correct'*, *'true'*) usually refer to discourse entities (Eckert and Strube, 2000). Other examples are certain types of complement constructions (like *'that is why/because/what/how'*), *'do-object'* expressions, which also may point at verbal antecedents (Müller, 2008). The inclusion of context may also be useful for capturing any tokens that point at abstract/concrete character of reference. The size of the context window was chosen intuitively, we did not conduct any separate experiments for finding the optimal window size, but may do it in the future.

Additional linguistic features used to represent anaphors $\rho(x)$ and antecedent candidates $\psi(y)$ are also different. Again, we use SpaCy to extract part of speech (POS) and dependency edge (DEP) tags for tokens in segments, and Berkeley Neural Parser (Kitaev et al., 2019) to get syntactic constituents (nominal, verbal, or other). We use POS and DEP tags for anaphors. According to our statistical findings (see Table 12 in AppendixA), there are some differences in distributions of (POS, DEP) combination depending on the mention type. E.g., the (PRON, nsubj) combination is especially frequent in case of discourse deictic anaphors, while (DET, det) is not. Our antecedent candidates encompass four additional features, of which only span width is borrowed from *coref-hoi*. Other features include span type (verbal, noun, other), POS and DEP tags of the last token. The span type feature was introduced based on the observation that discourse deictic anaphors mostly have verbal phrases or sentences as antecedents, and 'standard' anaphors - noun phrases. The other two features are meant to help identify discourse entities, which often encompass the whole sentence and thus end with a punctuation mark. Note that none of our shallow linguistic features is decisive. Moreover, both SpaCy and Berkeley Neural Parser may not function properly on dialogue data. Still, our experiments on the toy dataset (consisting of a single light_train 2022 file) show that without all these features the model is only able to achieve 29.41% CoNLL F1 score on the light_dev 2022 data. Adding features helps increase this score up to 36.44%.

All linguistic features described in this section

are represented as trainable embeddings of length 100.

3.4 Training

To train our model we kept the hyperparameters reported by *coref-hoi*, namely BERT- and task-specific learning rates (1e-5 and 3e-4, respectively), optimizers (AdamW and Adam), schedulers and dropout rate of 0.3. The number of training epochs was set to 24, but we had to stop training after 17 epochs. Currently the model is computationally inefficient (it is able to process only a single training example at a time), so we did not have enough time to complete the training.

The model was trained using a combination of several loss functions: (i) marginal log-likelihood of possibly correct antecedents; (ii) anaphor type loss checking how well the model distinguishes between discourse deixis, identity and non-referential anaphors; (iii) label loss that punishes the model if it tends to reject all antecedent candidates while having a referential anaphor; (iv) constituent type loss checking how well the model can differentiate between valid (verbal and nominal) and invalid (various fragments) antecedents. The addition of label loss is motivated by the fact that at early stages of training our model always tends to reject all antecedents by assigning negative scores to them. Constituent type loss is inspired by the mention loss in *coref-hoi*. The idea is that the model should assign larger scores to valid constituents. This loss is used with a coefficient $\lambda = 0.02$ to account for a big number of constituents and prevent it from dominating over all other losses.

3.5 Results and discussion

We used the same model for all three discourse deixis tracks. Table 7 illustrates the scores achieved by our model on the official test sets. Because the model is designed to resolve only four potential antecedents, there is no big difference in scores between the (Pred) and (Gold M) tracks. The scores for the latter are even slightly worse, as the model has to deal with numerous anaphor candidates it has not seen before. The best scores are reached for the (Gold A) track. It should be noted that here the model tries to resolve all annotated anaphors, not only the four target ones. Still, we tend to attribute the increase in performance not to a wider coverage of anaphors, but to the fact that the model does not have to classify the anaphor types.

Track	Light	AMI	Persuasion	Swbd.
Eval-DD (Pred)	36.82	50.09	47.04	n/a
Eval-DD (Gold M)	35.91	47.13	48.24	n/a
Eval-DD (Gold A)	44.95	56.54	62.79	n/a

Table 7: CoNLL F1 scores on the official test sets

Data	2021		2022	
	Our model	Winner	Our model	Winner
Light	48.04	42.7	36.82	37.09
AMI	40.34	35.4	50.09	53.31
Persuasion	56.68	39.6	47.04	54.59
Swbd.	n/a	35.4	n/a	49.76

Table 8: Model comparison: CoNLL F1 scores on official tests 2021 and 2022 for the Eval-DD (Pred) track

Table 8 shows the CoNLL F1 scores achieved by our system and the winning model on the official test data 2022 for the Eval-DD (Pred) track. Our model ranks second for all the datasets with a score difference ranging from 0.27 to 7.55 points. To compare our model with the baseline model by Kobayashi et al. (2021), we also evaluate it on the test partitions of Light, AMI and Persuasion datasets without gold annotations released for the CCST 2021. We see that our approach beats the baseline on all the datasets.

To see the limitations of our model and have a better understanding of what it can/cannot learn, we additionally evaluate it on the test partitions of Light, AMI and Persuasion datasets from CCST 2021 containing gold annotations. Our analysis (see Table 13 in Appendix A) shows that the model struggles with the anaphor type identification: out of 292 true discourse deictic *'this'*, *'that'*, *'it'* and *'which'* only 212 (72.6%) are classified as having the same type, 62 (21.25%) - as anaphoric, and 18 (6.16%) as non-referential ones. Interestingly, only one of all misclassified anaphors is linked to the correctly predicted antecedent. Also, all anaphors incorrectly classified as non-referential get associated with empty spans. At the same time the model successfully finds antecedents for 144 (67.92%) out of 212 correctly identified discourse deictic anaphors. It looks like anaphor type is important for the model to be able to perform resolution.

Looking at Table 13, we can conclude that our model also has difficulties finding split antecedents: 41 anaphors (14.04%) out of 292 refer to them, but our model only finds 7. In general, the model demonstrates a tendency to choose discourse deixis antecedents consisting of single sentences. We hypothesize that it happens for the following reasons. First, there are not enough training examples with split antecedents. Second, our model lacks mechanisms to capture relations between split antecedents making them a coherent piece relative to a discourse deictic anaphor.

The following points should also be emphasized. So far we have not evaluated the performance of our model separately for each of the four anaphor candidates. We have not analyzed the ability of our model to resolve identity anaphora. However, such analysis would be useful, so we plan on conducting it in the future. Also, using a lot of features slows down the training process. Therefore we are planning to perform experiments testing different combinations of features and various feature embeddings sizes. Additional experiments on how the usage of features influences the model trained on all available training data are also necessary. Furthermore, an investigation of the quality of the constituent types, POS and DEP tags would be beneficial, considering that we use SpaCy and Berkeley Neural Parser on dialogue data, while they were trained on text corpora.

4 Bridging Resolution

In this section we introduce our submission for the resolution of bridging references. We submitted to the Eval-Br (Gold A) track, in which gold mentions and anaphors are given. This reduces the problem to the selection of antecedent (from gold mention candidates) for each given anaphor.

Track	Resolution of bridging
Setting	Gold mentions and anaphors
Baseline	Higher order coreference resolution (Joshi et al., 2019)
Approach	Modify baseline to match setting: 1) Batch size from one document to one anaphor 2) Remove span enumeration step and simple pairwise scorer 3) Use cross entropy loss instead of marginal log-likelihood
Train data	AMI, Switchboard, Light, Persuasion, BASHI, ISNotes
Dev data	AMI, Light, Persuasion (dev splits)

Table 9: Bridging resolution: approach summary

4.1 Data

In addition to the shared task dialogue datasets of AMI (851 bridging instances across 7 documents), Switchboard (603 instances, 11 documents), Light (381 instances, 20 documents), and Persuasion (245 instances, 21 documents), we also utilize the bridging anaphora resolution datasets of BASHI (Rösiger, 2018) and ISNotes (Markert et al., 2012) to train our models. BASHI is a corpus of 50 Wall Street Journal articles, containing 57,709 tokens and 410 bridging pair annotations. ISNotes is a corpus of Wall Street Journal articles as well, containing 663 bridging pair annotations. The inclusion of these supplementary datasets was important, as the shared task datasets are relatively small, and the model architecture is fairly complex and expressive, making it easy to overfit.

4.2 Model architecture

Our approach is based on "independent" variant of the higher-order coreference architecture introduced in Joshi et al. (2019). We make a number of modifications to the architecture and training procedure (an overview of the original model/architecture can be found in Joshi et al. (2019) and the system it is built on, introduced in Lee et al. (2018). Note that the *coref-hoi* system proposed alternatives to the original higher-order system presented in Joshi et al. (2019), but these alternatives (such as the cluster merging model variant) are not relevant for our system, as we are not finding clusters of coreferent mentions.

Our modifications follow that of the bridging resolution system introduced in Renner et al. (2021). The first modification is a result of the gold anaphors being given: since we do not need to detect anaphors from the text, we can pass one anaphor at a time into the model (together with the document text and gold mentions) instead of passing the whole document at once and detecting and resolving potential anaphors. While this means potentially processing each document multiple times if there are multiple bridging anaphors in the document, this is done to decrease memory requirements significantly, as the pairwise scoring function is run for just one anaphor with its candidates, instead of many anaphors with all of their candidates. This decrease in memory usage allows for changes to the architecture that make it simpler and more accurate (see next paragraph). Also, in practice, the bridging datasets are relatively small, so this extra processing of the same document results in a negligible decrease in computational efficiency.

The architecture modifications are made possible by the decrease in memory usage allowed from having the mentions given and processing one anaphor at a time. Recall that in the original architecture by (Lee et al., 2018), they use a "two stage beam search" when detecting mentions and finding coreferent pairs: first, they prune potential mentions based on a span scoring function, then they prune antecedents for each span based on a "fast" bilinear scorer (the "coarse" part of the coarse-to-fine scorer), before sending the remaining spans and their list of antecedent candidates to the more computation- and memory-heavy "fine" scorer. This beam search was proposed to allow the system to scale better to longer documents. By having the gold mentions, we can remove the "fast" span scorer from the original model, as we no longer need to enumerate all possible spans. Also, since the pairwise memory restraints are reduced by passing just one anaphor into the model at a time, we can remove the "coarse" pairwise scorer and skip directly to the "fine" scorer. We make these changes in order to use the more expressive "fine" scorer directly on all pairs, without having to filter possible mentions and antecedents based on the less expressive 'fast" span scorer and "coarse" pairwise scorer.

After these modifications, the model architecture is as follows: pass entire document through the base contextual language model, obtain span representations for the gold mentions and anaphors, compute antecedents via the higher-order mechanism introduced in Lee et al. (2018). Also, this allows the use of cross entropy loss over all possible antecedents for each anaphor, instead of the original marginal log-likelihood, leading to a more direct optimization of the pairwise scorer.

We use `bert-base-uncased` as our base language model. We use this instead of `bert-large-uncased` because the resulting embedding is of smaller dimensionality, leading to less parameters in our token attention and span pair scoring layers. We experimented with the SpanBERT variant as well, but this led to slightly lower scores in preliminary experiments.

4.3 Training

We trained the system for 5 epochs on a single Tesla P100 GPU. The learning rate was set to 3e-3 and we used Adam optimizer. We froze the base BERT model to prevent overfitting as the dataset is relatively small even with the supplementary data, set the dropout to 0.3 in the fine tuning layers, and used a higher-order depth of 2. It took about 1 hour to complete training.

Switchboard	Light	Persuasion	AMI
35.78	37.68	50.99	35.23

Table 10: Test set results for the bridging task (gold anaphors)

4.4 Results and discussion

The submission Entity-F1 scores are shown in Table 10. Overall, we report scores slightly higher than reported in Renner et al. (2021) for bridging resolution, with scores on the Persuasion dataset being significantly higher than on the other three datasets. This setting allows for a more direct evaluation of the span embedding and pairwise scoring mechanisms from Joshi et al. (2019) and Lee et al. (2018), as we can remove steps in the fine tuning architecture that are only needed to manage memory usage. These results show the effectiveness of the span embedding and pairwise score on span comparisons tasks such as gold mention/anaphor bridging resolution.

5 Conclusion and Outlook

In this paper we presented our systems for identity anaphora, bridging and discourse deixis resolution.

Our system for the identity anaphora resolution combines the outputs of WCS and the *coref-hoi* system trained with "cluster merging". It ranked second in the shared task competition. When experimenting with WCS we tested different settings and tried replacing and adding different embeddings for mention representations (e.g., SpanBERT). However, the configuration reported in Anikina et al. (2021) turned out to work best on our development set. We also tested a combination of WCS trained on the shared task data and CCS trained on OntoNotes as well as *coref-hoi* trained on a combination of dialogue and non-dialogue datasets. The analysis of the model outputs shows that WCS works reasonably well for detecting singletons and pronominal clusters but performs worse when clustering noun phrases. Hence, we combine the outputs of WCS and the *coref-hoi* model and achieve an average improvement of 7.95% CoNLL score over vanilla clustering with WCS.

In the future we would like to do a more fine-grained analysis of the combined model outputs and test if one could use automatic coreference annotations from other pre-trained models as a weak supervision signal for WCS. In particular, we are interested in evaluating this model on the domain adaptation task and in the low resource setting. We would also like to perform more experiments with coreference chain editing based on the outputs of several models.

The system for discourse deixis resolution ranked second for all three tracks of the shared task. It was able to reach the CoNLL F1 scores ranging from 35.91% to 62.79% depending on the track and dataset. Some of these scores are close to the scores achieved by the winning team.

The model is based on a novel idea that it is possible to combine the tasks of discourse deixis and anaphora resolution. It is our first attempt at implementing this idea, so there is much space for improvement and additional analysis. First, we plan on making our model computationally more efficient, namely, we are going to perform some experiments with adaptive span pruning and check the influence of linguistic features given a larger training set. Second, it is possible to expand the set of potential anaphors. Before doing that, we need to analyse the ability of our model to resolve identity anaphora. Depending on the results, we may use our discourse deixis resolution model to enhance the coreference resolution performed by the WCS model. Finally, the phenomenon of split antecedents requires more investigation, namely, how we can model coherence/relations between them.

The system for the resolution of gold bridging anaphors is based on a higher order coreference system adapted for the setting. While the gold mentions/anaphors setting is much simpler than full bridging (mention/anaphor detection and resolution), the results show how well the span embedding and pairwise scoring mechanisms from Joshi et al. (2019) and Lee et al. (2018) work for bridging pairs.

Acknowledgements

The authors are supported by the German Ministry of Education and Research (BMBF): T. Anikina in project CORA4NLP (grant Nr. 01IW20010); N. Skachkova, P. Trivedi, J. Renner in IMPRESS (grant Nr. 01IS20076).

References

Anikina, T., Oguz, C., Skachkova, N., Tao, S., Upadhyaya, S., and Kruijff-Korbayova, I. (2021). Anaphora resolution in dialogue: Description of the DFKI-TalkingRobots system for the CODI-CRAC 2021 shared-task. In *Proceedings of the CODI-CRAC 2021 Shared Task on Anaphora, Bridging, and Discourse Deixis in Dialogue*, pages 32–42, Punta Cana, Dominican Republic. Association for Computational Linguistics.

Byron, D. K. (2002). *Resolving pronominal reference to abstract entities*. University of Rochester.

Devlin, J., Chang, M.-W., Lee, K., and Toutanova, K. (2018). BERT: Pre-training of deep bidirectional transformers for language understanding. *arXiv preprint arXiv:1810.04805*.

Eckert, M. and Strube, M. (2000). Dialogue acts, synchronizing units, and anaphora resolution. *Journal of Semantics*, 17(1):51–89.

Honnibal, M., Montani, I., Van Landeghem, S., and Boyd, A. (2020). SpaCy: Industrial-strength Natural Language Processing in Python.

Joshi, M., Levy, O., Zettlemoyer, L., and Weld, D. (2019). BERT for coreference resolution: Baselines and analysis. In *Proceedings of the 2019 Conference on Empirical Methods in Natural Language Processing and the 9th International Joint Conference on Natural Language Processing (EMNLP-IJCNLP)*, pages 5803–5808, Hong Kong, China. Association for Computational Linguistics.

Khosla, S., Yu, J., Manuvinakurike, R., Ng, V., Poesio, M., Strube, M., and Rosé, C. (2021). The CODI-CRAC 2021 shared task on anaphora, bridging, and discourse deixis in dialogue. In *Proceedings of the CODI-CRAC 2021 Shared Task on Anaphora, Bridging, and Discourse Deixis in Dialogue*, pages 1–15, Punta Cana, Dominican Republic. Association for Computational Linguistics.

Kim, H., Kim, D., and Kim, H. (2021). The pipeline model for resolution of anaphoric reference and resolution of entity reference. In *Proceedings of the CODI-CRAC 2021 Shared Task on Anaphora, Bridging, and Discourse Deixis in Dialogue*, pages 43–47, Punta Cana, Dominican Republic. Association for Computational Linguistics.

Kitaev, N., Cao, S., and Klein, D. (2019). Multilingual constituency parsing with self-attention and pre-training. In *Proceedings of the 57th Annual Meeting of the Association for Computational Linguistics*, pages 3499–3505, Florence, Italy. Association for Computational Linguistics.

Kobayashi, H., Li, S., and Ng, V. (2021). Neural anaphora resolution in dialogue. In *Proceedings of the CODI-CRAC 2021 Shared Task on Anaphora, Bridging, and Discourse Deixis in Dialogue*, pages 16–31, Punta Cana, Dominican Republic. Association for Computational Linguistics.

Kolhatkar, V., Roussel, A., Dipper, S., and Zinsmeister, H. (2018). Anaphora With Non-nominal Antecedents in Computational Linguistics: a Survey. *Computational Linguistics*, 44(3):547–612.

Lee, K., He, L., and Zettlemoyer, L. (2018). Higher-order coreference resolution with coarse-to-fine inference. In *Proceedings of the 2018 Conference of the North American Chapter of the Association for Computational Linguistics: Human Language Technologies, Volume 2 (Short Papers)*, pages 687–692, New Orleans, Louisiana. Association for Computational Linguistics.

Markert, K., Hou, Y., and Strube, M. (2012). Collective classification for fine-grained information status. In *Proceedings of the 50th Annual Meeting of the Association for Computational Linguistics (Volume 1: Long Papers)*, pages 795–804, Jeju Island, Korea. Association for Computational Linguistics.

Müller, M.-C. (2008). *Fully automatic resolution of'it','this', and'that'in unrestricted multi-party dialog*. PhD thesis, Universität Tübingen.

Navarretta, C. (2004). Resolving individual and abstract anaphora in texts and dialogues. In *COLING 2004: Proceedings of the 20th International Conference on Computational Linguistics*, pages 233–239, Geneva, Switzerland. COLING.

Pennington, J., Socher, R., and Manning, C. D. (2014). Glove: Global vectors for word representation. In *Proceedings of the 2014 conference on empirical methods in natural language processing (EMNLP)*, pages 1532–1543.

Pradhan, S., Moschitti, A., Xue, N., Uryupina, O., and Zhang, Y. (2012). CoNLL-2012 shared task: Modeling multilingual unrestricted coreference in OntoNotes. In *Joint Conference on EMNLP and CoNLL - Shared Task*, pages 1–40, Jeju Island, Korea. Association for Computational Linguistics.

Renner, J., Trivedi, P., Maheshwari, G., Gilleron, R., and Denis, P. (2021). An end-to-end approach for full bridging resolution. In *Proceedings of the CODI-CRAC 2021 Shared Task on Anaphora, Bridging, and Discourse Deixis in Dialogue*, pages 48–54, Punta Cana, Dominican Republic. Association for Computational Linguistics.

Rocha, M. (1999). Coreference resolution in dialogues in English and Portuguese. In *Coreference and Its Applications*.

Rösiger, I. (2018). BASHI: A corpus of Wall Street Journal articles annotated with bridging links. In *Proceedings of the Eleventh International Conference on Language Resources and Evaluation (LREC 2018)*, Miyazaki, Japan. European Language Resources Association (ELRA).

Speer, R., Chin, J., and Havasi, C. (2017). ConceptNet 5.5: An Open Multilingual Graph of General Knowledge. In *Proceedings of the Thirty-First AAAI Conference on Artificial Intelligence*, AAAI'17, page 4444–4451. AAAI Press.

Strube, M. and Müller, C. (2003). A machine learning approach to pronoun resolution in spoken dialogue. In *Proceedings of the 41st Annual Meeting of the Association for Computational Linguistics*, pages 168–175, Sapporo, Japan. Association for Computational Linguistics.

Wang, W., Wei, F., Dong, L., Bao, H., Yang, N., and Zhou, M. (2020). MiniLM: Deep Self-Attention Distillation for Task-Agnostic Compression of Pre-Trained Transformers. In *Advances in Neural Information Processing Systems 33: Annual Conference on Neural Information Processing Systems 2020, NeurIPS 2020, December 6-12, 2020, virtual*.

Webber, B. L. (1988). Discourse deixis and discourse processing.

Xu, L. and Choi, J. D. (2020). Revealing the myth of higher-order inference in coreference resolution. In *Proceedings of the 2020 Conference on Empirical Methods in Natural Language Processing (EMNLP)*, pages 8527–8533, Online. Association for Computational Linguistics.

Xu, L. and Choi, J. D. (2021). Adapted end-to-end coreference resolution system for anaphoric identities in dialogues. In *Proceedings of the CODI-CRAC 2021 Shared Task on Anaphora, Bridging, and Discourse Deixis in Dialogue*, pages 55–62, Punta Cana, Dominican Republic. Association for Computational Linguistics.

Yu, J., Khosla, S., Manuvinakurike, R., Levin, L., Ng, V., Poesio, M., Strube, M., and Rosé, C. (2022). The CODI-CRAC 2022 shared task on anaphora, bridging, and discourse deixis in dialogue. In *Proceedings of the CODI-CRAC 2022 Shared Task on Anaphora, Bridging, and Discourse Deixis in Dialogue*.

A Appendix: Discourse Deixis

Here we present statistical findings used to pick out features to represent anaphor candidates. Table 11 shows the relative frequencies of parent tokens' lemmas for three types of 'anaphors': discourse deictic, anaphoric and non-referential. Table 12 illustrates the joint distribution of POS and DEP labels of possible anaphor candidates, also depending on their type. All numbers were extracted from the CCST 2021 training data, namely ARRAU, Light, AMI, Persuasion, and Switchboard.

	Anaphor's parent					
	DD		ID		non-ref	
Lemma	s	0.329	be	0.139	be	0.202
	be	0.235	s	0.117	s	0.078
	do	0.040	have	0.048	have	0.031
	about	0.037	do	0.038	like	0.022
	sound	0.020	use	0.027	make	0.022
	like	0.020	...		...	
	...					
	have	0.017				
	...					
	make	0.013				
	...					
	use	0.003				

Table 11: Distribution of anaphors' parents depending on the anaphors' types

	Mention					
	DD		ID		non-ref	
POS+DEP	(PRON, nsubj)	0.664	(PRON, nsubj)	0.46	(PRON, nsubj)	0.390
	(PRON, dobj)	0.148	(PRON, dobj)	0.249	(SCONJ, mark)	0.173
	(PRON, pobj)	0.117	(DET, det)	0.139	(DET, det)	0.138
	(DET, det)	0.03	(PRON, pobj)	0.074	(PRON, pobj)	0.110
	(PRON, mark)	0.013	(PRON, dep)	0.02	(PRON, dobj)	0.097

Table 12: Distribution of anaphors' POS and dependency edges tags depending on the anaphors' types

Table 13 presents an error analysis of our discourse deixis resolution model on the test Light, AMI and Persuasion data from CCST 2021. We analyze the antecedent predictions made by our model as follows. If they are not empty, all predicted antecedents are divided into split and not split, depending on a simple heuristics: if a predicted sequence of (sub)tokens (the very last token is always excluded) contains a dot, a question or an exclamation mark), it is considered to be split. Next, we check if the antecedents' borders are correct. Here, four cases are possible: (i) only the left border is wrong; (ii) only the right border is wrong; (iii) both borders are wrong; (iv) both borders are correct.

The table also shows the anaphor type predicted by the model for all 292 gold discourse deictic anaphors.

		Gold ant. not spl.			Gold ant. spl.		
	Predictions	non-ref	DD	ID	non-ref	DD	ID
not split	left border wr.	0	3	3	0	16	0
	right border wr.	0	1	2	0	0	1
	all borders wr.	0	34	45	0	4	7
	all borders cor.	0	137	0	0	0	0
split	left border wr.	0	1	0	0	2	0
	right border wr.	0	3	0	0	0	0
	all borders wr.	0	0	0	0	0	0
	all borders cor.	0	0	0	0	7	1
	empty	16	3	3	2	1	0

Table 13: Performance on the test partitions of AMI, Light & Persuasion datasets from CODI-CRAC 2021 Shared Task

Pipeline Coreference Resolution Model for Anaphoric Identity in Dialogues

Damrin Kim*, **Seongsik Park**, **Mirae Han** and **Harksoo Kim**
Department of Artificial Intelligence, Konkuk University, Seoul, Republic of Korea
{ekafls33, a163912, future26, nlpdrkim}@konkuk.ac.kr

Abstract

CODI-CRAC 2022 Shared Task in Dialogues consists of three sub-tasks: Sub-task 1 is the resolution of anaphoric identity, sub-task 2 is the resolution of bridging references, and sub-task 3 is the resolution of discourse deixis/abstract anaphora. Anaphora resolution is the task of detecting mentions from input documents and clustering the mentions of the same entity. The end-to-end model proceeds with the pruning of the candidate mention, and the pruning has the possibility of removing the correct mention. Also, the end-to-end anaphora resolution model has high model complexity, which takes a long time to train. Therefore, we proceed with the anaphora resolution as a two-stage pipeline model. In the first mention detection step, the score of the candidate word span is calculated, and the mention is predicted without pruning. In the second anaphora resolution step, the pair of mentions of the anaphora resolution relationship is predicted using the mentions predicted in the mention detection step. We propose a two-stage anaphora resolution pipeline model that reduces model complexity and training time, and maintains similar performance to end-to-end models. As a result of the experiment, the anaphora resolution showed a performance of 68.27% in Light, 48.87% in AMI, 69.06% in Persuasion, and 60.99% on Switchboard. Our final system ranked 3rd on the leaderboard of sub-task 1.

1 Introduction

Anaphora resolution(Kim et al., 2021; Yu et al., 2022) is the task of detecting mentions from input documents and clustering the mentions of the same entity. It is used for various natural language processing tasks such as document summarization, question answering, and knowledge extraction. Mention detection is the task of extracting candidate word spans that are likely to be mentions within a sentence. Mention refers to a span of candidate words that are highly likely to have a anaphora relationship in a sentence. Most of the anaphora resolution models being studied recently are end-to-end models. The end-to-end model extracts and learns all candidate word spans that are likely to be a mention and prunes them at a fixed ratio. The mention pairs are made from pruned mentions and are clustered into final mention pairs based on calculated scores. However, fixing the prune ratio is inefficient. A high pruning ratio increases the number of non-correct candidate mentions, increasing the amount and complexity of calculations. Conversely, a low ratio increases the possibility of removing correct answers instead of lowering the amount and complexity. Finding the optimal pruning ratio is important because the pruning ratio of the mention detection can directly affect the anaphora resolution performance. Therefore, we propose a two-stage anaphora resolution pipeline model to speed up training and reduce model complexity without pruning. Table 1 summarizes the description of the system and experiment.

In the first mention detection step, the mention is trained by calculating scores of all possible candidate word spans in the input sentence. In the second anaphora resolution step, a mention pair consists of the mentions predicted in the detection step. Then, the mention pair score is calculated to train the mention pair, which is a anaphora relationship. The proposed model shows high performance in the mention detection. Moreover, compared with the self-reimplemented end-to-end anaphora resolution model, it shows similar performance and fast training speed.

2 Related Works

Recently, anaphora resolution has been studied using an end-to-end model that learns pairwise scores of entity mentions(Lee et al., 2017). The end-to-end model calculate mention score with all possible spans in a given text. The pruning step proceeds

Proceedings of the CODI-CRAC 2022 Shared Task on Anaphora, Bridging, and Discourse Deixis in Dialogue, pages 28–31
Gyeongju, Republic of Korea, October 17, 2022.
https://doi.org/10.26615/978-954-452-056-4_003

Track	Resolution of anaphoric identities
Setting	Predicted mentions
Baseline	-
Approach	Sec. 3.1 and 3.2
Train Data	Sec. 4.1
Dev Data	Sec. 4.1

Table 1: System summary

with the calculated mention scores. The anaphora score is calculated by a pair of mentions made with current and antecedent mentions(Lee et al., 2018; Devlin et al., 2018; Joshi et al., 2020).

Before Dobrovolskii (2021) was introduced, the end-to-end models mainly achieved a state-of-the-art anaphora resolution. Dobrovolskii (2021) proceeded with a pipeline to resolve anaphora resolution. As a result, they reduced the complexity of the model from $O(n^4)$ to $O(n^2)$ and improved its performance. Unlike the existing end-to-end models, it is possible to efficiently detect mentions because it does not calculate mention scores and perform the pruning step. We propose a two-stage anaphora resolution model that utilizes not only the information of the current speaker but also of the previous speaker, considering the anaphora resolution characteristics of the dialogue domain. The proposed model is faster in training and evaluation compared to end-to-end models.

3 Model

3.1 Mention Detection

The mention detection model consists of a pre-trained language model, a mention representation generation layer, and a mention score generation layer.

$$X = \{x_1, x_2, \cdots, x_T\} \quad (1)$$

Pre-trained language model receives input tokens in a sentence and outputs the token representation X. T denotes the number of tokens. $N = T(T+1)/2$ is the number of possible text spans.

$$g_m(i) = [x_{START(i)}, x_{END(i)}] \quad (2)$$

Mention representation $g_m(i)$ is generated by connecting $START(i)$ and $END(i)$, which are the start and end index token representations of span i. The mention score $S_m(i)$ is calculated through FNN(feed-forward neural network):

$$S_m(i) = W_m \cdot FNN_m(g_m(i)) \quad (3)$$

$S_m(i)$ is calculated by multiplying the mention representation by the learnable weight W_m. It trains to minimize the cross-entropy between predicted and correct mentions, as follows:

$$loss_m = -\sum_i Y_i^m log\left(\hat{Y}_i^m\right) \quad (4)$$

3.2 Anaphora Resolution

Anaphora resolution model can be divided into a pre-trained language model, a mention representation generation layer, and a pairwise score generation layer. The pre-trained language model receives input tokens in a document and outputs the token representation X. D denotes the number of tokens in the document. We segment a document into the maximum size of pre-trained language model to process documents that are longer than this. The segmented documents are used independently as input. The outputs of the pre-trained language model are concatenated and reconstructed to be a document.

$$X = \{x_1, x_2, ..., x_D\} \quad (5)$$

Mention representation $g_c(i)$ is generated using the predicted mentions in the mention detection model. The token representations of span boundaries, the average of token representations in span, and the feature vector are concatenated to generate $g_c(i)$. The feature vector $\phi(i)$ contains speaker information of current and previous sentences and is initialized by random embedding. This helps eliminate the ambiguity of personal pronouns such as 'you' and 'I' when there are multiple speakers.

$$\begin{aligned} g_c(i) = [&x_{START(i)}, x_{END(i)} \\ &, avg(x_{START(i)}; x_{END(i)}), \phi(i)] \end{aligned} \quad (6)$$

Mention pair uses mention representations to generate all possible pairs without duplicate ones. Next, pairwise score $S_c(i,j)$ is calculated through FNN by connecting $g_c(i)$ and $g_c(j)$, which are mention representation pairs:

$$S_c(i,j) = W_c \cdot FNN_c(g_c(i), g_c(j)) \quad (7)$$

$S_c(i)$ is calculated by multiplying the mention representation pair by the learnable weight W_c. It trains to minimize the cross-entropy between predicted pairwise scores of mention pairs and correct mention pairs:

$$loss_c = -\sum_i Y_i^c log\left(\hat{Y}_i^c\right) \quad (8)$$

4 Experiments

4.1 Datasets

We use datasets provided by CODICRAC 2022 Shared-Task for learning and evaluation. We use the train and dev dataset of Light, AMI, Persuasion, Switchboard and train, dev, and test dataset of ARRAU for training, and use the test dataset of Light, AMI, Persuasion, and Switchboard for evaluation. All datasets are dialogue domains and consist of Universal Anaphora(Poesio et al., 2004) annotations. The statistics of the datasets used for training and validation are shown in Table 2 and 3. #D is the total number of documents, #S is the total number of sentences, #W is the total number of words, #M is the total number of mentions, #C is the total number of clusters, and #SPK is the average number of speakers per document.

	Light	AMI	PSUA	SWBD	ARRAU
#D	20	7	21	11	202
#S	909	4,140	813	1,343	4,230
#W	11,495	33,741	9,185	14,992	110,440
#M	3,907	8,918	2,743	4,024	34,454
#C	1,803	4,391	1,513	2,362	23,238
#SPK	2,95	4	2	2	-

Table 2: Statistics for train datasets.

	Light	AMI	PSUA	SWBD	ARRAU
#D	21	3	27	22	18
#S	924	1,968	1,110	3,653	479
#W	11,824	18,260	12,198	35,027	12,845
#M	3,941	4,870	3,697	9,392	3,961
#C	1,789	2,551	1,996	5,436	2,640
#SPK	3	4	2	2	-

Table 3: Statistics for dev datasets.

4.2 Evaluation Metrics

The Mention Detection Model measures performance using F1-score, the harmonic mean of precision and recall, as follows:

$$\begin{aligned} Precision &= \frac{True\,Positive}{True\,Positive + False\,Positive} \\ Recall &= \frac{True\,Positive}{True\,Positive + False\,Negative} \\ F1 - score &= \frac{2 * Precision * Recall}{Precision + Recall} \end{aligned} \tag{9}$$

The evaluation of the anaphora resolution model is conducted with the SemEval evaluation program. We measure CoNLL F1 score(Pradhan et al., 2014) which averages three performances in the official evaluation process since CoNLL-2011: B3(Bagga and Baldwin, 1998), a mention-based method, CEAFe(Luo, 2005), an entity-based method and MUC(Vilain et al., 1995), a link-based method.

4.3 Experiments on Mention Detection

As shown in Table 4, our mention detection model shows F1 performance of 92.17% on Light, 80.46% on AMI, 89.67% on Persuasion(PSUA), and 85.02% on Switchboard(SWBD).

	Precision	Recall	F1-score
Light	94.76	89.72	92.17
AMI	88.15	74.01	80.46
PSUA	90.67	88.70	89.67
SWBD	92.60	78.58	85.02

Table 4: Results on mention detection for test datasets.

4.4 Experiments on Anaphora Resolution

As shown in Table 5, our anaphora resolution model shows a CoNLL F1 performance of 68.27% on Light, 48.87% on AMI, 69.06% on Persuasion, and 60.99% on Switchboard.

		Light	AMI	PUSA	SWBD
	P	73.45	36.05	70.04	53.83
MUC	R	83.31	77.67	83.23	83.12
	F1	78.07	49.24	76.07	65.34
	P	76.72	46.22	70.00	58.46
B^3	R	55.14	64.06	69.97	69.08
	F1	64.16	53.70	69.99	63.33
	P	63.08	70.76	76.31	70.73
$CEAF_e$	R	62.07	31.57	51.00	44.07
	F1	62.27	43.66	61.14	54.31
CoNLL F1	F1	68.27	48.87	69.06	60.99

Table 5: Results on anaphora resolution for test datasets.

In Table 6, the proposed model shows similar performance to the self-implemented end-to-end anaphora resolution model(Lee et al., 2017).

We also show the effectiveness of the two-stage pipeline model because the model complexity is reduced from $O(n^4)$ to $O(n^2)$, and the total training time is reduced by about 1/10.

model	Light	AMI	PSUA	SWBD
end-to-end	70.45	35.34	67.52	61.27
ours	68.27	48.87	69.06	60.99

Table 6: CoNLL F1-score of pipeline(proposed model) and end-to-end model

5 Conclusion

We propose a pipeline model for anaphora resolution. Our proposed model consists of a mention detection model and an anaphora resolution model. The mention detection model predicts mentions by the span prediction method. The anaphora resolution model predicts a pair of mentions of an anaphora relation by the mention pair method based on results from the mention detection model. In subtask 1, our model achieved 68.3%, 48.8%, 69.1%, and 61.0% performance on Light, AMI, Persuasion, and Switchboard (ranked in the top 3). We will study a mention detection model robust in noun phrases by reflecting the context of the document and an anaphora resolution model by using GNN to reflect structural information between mentions.

Acknowledgements

This work was supported by Institute of Information & communications Technology Planning & Evaluation(IITP) grant funded by the Korea government(MSIT)(No.2020-0-00368, A Neural-Symbolic Model for Knowledge Acquisition and Inference Techniques)

References

Amit Bagga and Breck Baldwin. 1998. Algorithms for scoring coreference chains. In *The first international conference on language resources and evaluation workshop on linguistics coreference*, volume 1, pages 563–566. Citeseer.

Jacob Devlin, Ming-Wei Chang, Kenton Lee, and Kristina Toutanova. 2018. Bert: Pre-training of deep bidirectional transformers for language understanding. *arXiv preprint arXiv:1810.04805*.

Vladimir Dobrovolskii. 2021. Word-level coreference resolution. *arXiv preprint arXiv:2109.04127*.

Mandar Joshi, Danqi Chen, Yinhan Liu, Daniel S Weld, Luke Zettlemoyer, and Omer Levy. 2020. Spanbert: Improving pre-training by representing and predicting spans. *Transactions of the Association for Computational Linguistics*, 8:64–77.

Hongjin Kim, Damrin Kim, and Harksoo Kim. 2021. The pipeline model for resolution of anaphoric reference and resolution of entity reference. In *Proceedings of the CODI-CRAC 2021 Shared Task on Anaphora, Bridging, and Discourse Deixis in Dialogue*, pages 43–47.

Kenton Lee, Luheng He, Mike Lewis, and Luke Zettlemoyer. 2017. End-to-end neural coreference resolution. *arXiv preprint arXiv:1707.07045*.

Kenton Lee, Luheng He, and Luke Zettlemoyer. 2018. Higher-order coreference resolution with coarse-to-fine inference. *arXiv preprint arXiv:1804.05392*.

Xiaoqiang Luo. 2005. On coreference resolution performance metrics. In *Proceedings of Human Language Technology Conference and Conference on Empirical Methods in Natural Language Processing*, pages 25–32.

Massimo Poesio, Rahul Mehta, Axel Maroudas, and Janet Hitzeman. 2004. Learning to resolve bridging references. In *Proceedings of the 42nd Annual Meeting of the Association for Computational Linguistics (ACL-04)*, pages 143–150.

Sameer Pradhan, Xiaoqiang Luo, Marta Recasens, Eduard Hovy, Vincent Ng, and Michael Strube. 2014. Scoring coreference partitions of predicted mentions: A reference implementation. In *Proceedings of the conference. Association for Computational Linguistics. Meeting*, volume 2014, page 30. NIH Public Access.

Marc Vilain, John D Burger, John Aberdeen, Dennis Connolly, and Lynette Hirschman. 1995. A model-theoretic coreference scoring scheme. In *Sixth Message Understanding Conference (MUC-6): Proceedings of a Conference Held in Columbia, Maryland, November 6-8, 1995*.

Juntao Yu, Sopan Khosla, Ramesh Manuvinakurike, Vincent Ng, Massimo Poesio, Michael Strube, and Carolyn Rosé. 2022. The codi-crac 2022 shared task on anaphora, bridging, and discourse deixis in dialogue. In *Proceedings of the CODI-CRAC 2022 Shared Task on Anaphora, Bridging, and Discourse Deixis in Dialogue*.

Neural Anaphora Resolution in Dialogue Revisited

Shengjie Li and **Hideo Kobayashi** and **Vincent Ng**
Human Language Technology Research Institute
University of Texas at Dallas
Richardson, TX 75083-0688
{sxl180006,hideo,vince}@hlt.utdallas.edu

Abstract

We present the systems that we developed for all three tracks of the CODI-CRAC 2022 shared task, namely the anaphora resolution track, the bridging resolution track, and the discourse deixis resolution track. Combining an effective encoding of the input using the $\text{SpanBERT}_{\text{Large}}$ encoder with an extensive hyperparameter search process, our systems achieved the highest scores in all phases of all three tracks.

1 Introduction

Following the CODI-CRAC 2021 shared task (Khosla et al., 2021), the CODI-CRAC 2022 shared task (Yu et al., 2022) focuses on resolving anaphoric references in dialogue. The two shared tasks are structured in more or less the same way. Specifically, in order to track progress on resolving anaphoric references in dialogue made over the past year, this year's shared task has essentially the same format as last year's, except that a new Gold Anaphor (Gold A) phase is added to both the bridging resolution track and the discourse deixis resolution track. By providing the participants with gold anaphors, the Gold A phase allows participants to focus on antecedent selection, thus making it easier to compare different systems' resolution performances.

Similar to last year, this year we participated and ranked first in all phases of all three tracks. We believe that our success can largely be attributed to two factors. First, leveraging the successes achieved by span-based models in last year's shared task (Kobayashi et al., 2021; Xu and Choi, 2021), we employ $\text{SpanBERT}_{\text{Large}}$ (Joshi et al., 2020) as our encoder in all three tracks. Second, we combine the resulting effective encoding of the input documents with an extensive hyperparameter search process. More specifically:

- for anaphora resolution, we employ a three-step pipeline approach consisting of mention extraction, entity coreference resolution, and removal of non-referring and non-entity mentions, pretraining the mention extraction component and the entity coreference component on the OntoNotes 5.0 corpus;
- for discourse deixis resolution, we propose a number of task-specific extensions to the span-based model we used in last year's shared task (Kobayashi et al., 2021) that involve heuristically extracting candidate anaphors and antecedents, exploiting different types of features, and performing distance-based filtering of candidate antecedents;
- for bridging resolution, we extend Yu and Poesio's (2020) multi-task learning framework, which jointly identifies bridging and coreference links, by replacing its LSTM encoder with $\text{SpanBERT}_{\text{Large}}$ and employing a *turn* distance feature.

A brief overview of the approaches we adopted for the three tracks can be found in Table 1.

The rest of the paper is structured as follows. The next three sections describe our work for the three tracks, namely entity coreference (Section 2, discourse deixis (Section 3), and bridging (Section 4). In each section, we describe our approach, our official results, and a brief analysis of the results, particularly a discussion of the impact of hyperparameter tuning on model performance. Finally, we present our conclusions in Section 5.

2 Anaphora Resolution

Last year we built a span-based entity coreference model for the Anaphora Resolution track that achieved competitive performance (Kobayashi et al., 2021). Since this year's Anaphora Resolution track has the exact same format as last year's, we developed this year's model based on last year's model (henceforth $\texttt{UTD}^{2021}$). Recall that $\texttt{UTD}^{2021}$ is an extension of Xu and Choi's (2020)

Proceedings of the CODI-CRAC 2022 Shared Task on Anaphora, Bridging, and Discourse Deixis in Dialogue, pages 32–47
Gyeongju, Republic of Korea, October 17, 2022. ©2022 Association for Computational Linguistics
https://doi.org/10.26615/978-954-452-056-4_004

	Entity Coreference Resolution
Baseline	Kobayashi et al.'s (2021) implementation of Xu and Choi.'s (2020) span-based model
Learning framework	A pipeline architecture consisting of a mention detection component, an entity coreference component, and a non-entity and non-referring mention removal component. The coreference component extends the baseline by (1) removing the type prediction model; and (2) rescoring the dummy antecedent at inference time to adjust the likelihood it will be selected as the antecedent.
Markable extraction	A mention detection model (adapted from Kobayashi et al. (2021)) is trained to identify the entity mentions.
Training data	The first two steps of our pipelined approach are pretrained on OntoNotes 5.0. All three steps of our pipelined approach are trained on ARRAU 3.0 (RST, GNOME, TRAINS91, TRAINS93, PEAR, $\text{LIGHT}_{\text{train}}$, $\text{AMI}_{\text{train}}$, $\text{Persuasion}_{\text{train}}$, $\text{Switchboard}_{\text{train}}$).
Development data	For all three steps, $\text{LIGHT}_{\text{dev}}$, AMI_{dev}, $\text{Persuasion}_{\text{dev}}$, and $\text{Switchboard}_{\text{dev}}$ are used. Note that after parameters are tuned on the dev data, we retrain the models on the combined training and dev sets using the tuned parameters before continuing parameter tuning on the test data. See Section 2.4.3 for details.
	Discourse Deixis Resolution
Baseline	Xu and Choi's (2020) implementation of Lee et al.'s (2018) span-based model
Learning framework	An extension of Xu and Choi's model with (1) heuristic extraction of candidate anaphors and antecedents, (2) an anaphor prediction model with which only those spans predicted as anaphors will be resolved, (3) a large-scale expansion of statistical features, and (4) filtering of candidate antecedents based on their distances from the anaphor under consideration. The models developed for the three phases differ w.r.t. the candidate anaphors they are trained on: in the Predicted phase, the model is trained on heuristically extracted candidate anaphors; in the Gold Mention phase, the model is trained on gold mentions; and in the Gold Anaphor phase, the model is trained on gold anaphors with gold mentions as their candidate antecedents.
Markable extraction	For the Predicted phase, markables are heuristically extracted. For the Gold Mention and Gold Anaphor phases, gold mentions and gold anaphors are used as candidate anaphors respectively. For all phases, candidate antecedents are extracted heuristically (utterances).
Training data	ARRAU 3.0 (RST, GNOME, TRAINS91, TRAINS93, PEAR, $\text{LIGHT}_{\text{train}}$, $\text{LIGHT}_{\text{dev}}$, $\text{AMI}_{\text{train}}$, AMI_{dev}, $\text{Persuasion}_{\text{train}}$, $\text{Persuasion}_{\text{dev}}$, $\text{Switchboard}_{\text{train}}$, $\text{Switchboard}_{\text{dev}}$).
Development data	None: we perform parameter tuning directly on the test data.
	Bridging Resolution
Baseline	Yu and Poesio's (2020) multi-task learning (MTL) framework
Learning framework	An extension of Yu and Poesio's framework in which we (1) replace their LSTM encoder with the $\text{SpanBERT}_{\text{Large}}$ encoder and (2) add a *turn* distance feature. The model for the Predicted phase and the Gold Mention phrase are both trained on automatically identified spans, while the model for the Gold Anaphor phase is trained on gold anaphors.
Markable extraction	For the Predicted phase, we employ the same mention extractor that we trained for the Anaphora Resolution track. For the Gold Mention and Gold Anaphor phases, gold mentions and gold anaphors are used as candidate anaphors respectively whereas gold mentions are used as candidate antecedents.
Training data	Three setups: (1) train on all of ARRAU 3.0; (2) pretrain on non-dialogue datasets (RST, GNOME, TRAINS91, TRAINS93), then train on data from the target (i.e., dialogue) domain ($\text{LIGHT}_{\text{train}}$, $\text{LIGHT}_{\text{dev}}$, $\text{AMI}_{\text{train}}$, AMI_{dev}, $\text{Persuasion}_{\text{train}}$, $\text{Persuasion}_{\text{dev}}$, $\text{Switchboard}_{\text{train}}$, $\text{Switchboard}_{\text{dev}}$); and (3) for each target dataset (e.g., LIGHT), first pretrain on non-dialogue datasets (RST, GNOME, TRAINS91, TRAINS93), then train on only the train split and the development split of the target dataset.
Development data	None: we perform parameter tuning directly on the test data.

Table 1: Overview of the approaches we adopted for the three tracks.

`coref-hoi` model. In order to help the reader understand the entity coreference model we employ for this year's shared task, we will begin by providing an overview of `coref-hoi` and UTD^{2021}.

2.1 `coref-hoi`

`coref-hoi` (Xu and Choi, 2020) is a re-implementation of the widely-used end-to-end coreference model by Lee et al. (2018). This model enumerates spans of up to a predefined length and, for computational efficiency reasons, generates a cultivated list of candidate mention spans that contains only a certain fraction n of the top spans, where n is a parameter known as the top span ratio. For each candidate mention span x, the model learns a distribution $P(y)$ over its candidate antecedents $y \in \mathcal{Y}(x)$. To maintain computational tractability, $\mathcal{Y}(x)$ contains only the top-k candidate antecedents (computed using the scoring function s_c, as described below) and a dummy antecedent ϵ, which should be selected when x does not have a coreferring mention preceding it in the associated text.

More specifically, $P(y)$ is computed as follows:

$$P(y) = \frac{e^{s(x,y)}}{\sum_{y' \in \mathcal{Y}(x)} e^{s(x,y')}}$$

where $s(x, y)$ is a pair-wise score that incorporates

two types of scores: (1) $s_m(\cdot)$, a score that corresponds to the probability of a span being a mention, (2) $s_c(\cdot)$ and $s_a(\cdot)$, scores that correspond to the probability of two spans referring to the same entity ($s(x, \epsilon) = 0$ for dummy antecedents):

$$s(x, y) = s_m(x) + s_m(y) + s_c(x, y) + s_a(x, y)$$
$$s_m(x) = \texttt{FFNN}_m(g_x)$$
$$s_c(x, y) = g_x^\top W_c g_y$$
$$s_a(x, y) = \texttt{FFNN}_c(g_x, g_y, g_x \circ g_y, \phi(x, y))$$

where g_x and g_y denote the vector representations of x and y, W_c is a learned weight matrix for bilinear scoring, FFNN$(\cdot)$ denotes a feedforward neural network, $\phi(\cdot)$ encodes the distance between two spans as well as the meta-information such as speaker information.

While $s_c(\cdot)$ and $s_a(\cdot)$ both attempt to score a candidate antecedent given a candidate anaphor, $s_a(\cdot)$ is supposed to provide more accurate candidate antecedent scores. The reason is that $s_a(\cdot)$ is calculated using an FFNN while $s_c(\cdot)$ is a far less accurate bilinear scoring function. Nevertheless, $s_c(\cdot)$ is much more efficient to compute than $s_a(\cdot)$. Given its efficiency, $s_c(\cdot)$ is being used to score *all* candidate antecedents (i.e., all the spans preceding the candidate anaphor), and only the top-k scoring spans are used to compute $P(y)$ (where k is a tunable parameter). In other words, the computationally expensive-to-compute $s_a(\cdot)$ function only needs to be applied to the top-k candidate antecedents for each candidate anaphor.

2.2 UTD^{2021}

UTD^{2021} has the following four important extensions to coref-hoi:

Type prediction model Motivated in part by our previous work (Lu and Ng, 2020), we employ a type prediction model in UTD^{2021} that takes as input the span embedding g_x and computes the probability that span x has type t (i.e., $ot_x(t)$). The span type t_x is determined by the type with the highest probability. UTD^{2021} classifies each span into two types, NULL and ENTITY, where ENTITY covers both referring and non-referring mentions and NULL covers the spans that do not correspond to entities.

$$ot_x = \texttt{FFNN}_t(g_x)$$
$$t_x = \arg\max_t ot_x(t)$$

A cross-entropy loss is computed using ot_x, which is then multiplied by a type loss coefficient and added to the loss function of coref-hoi. Specifically:

$$Loss = \lambda L_t + L_c$$

where L_t and L_c are the type prediction loss and the entity coreference loss respectively, and λ is the type loss coefficient, which specifies the relative importance of the two losses. In other words, UTD^{2021} jointly learns type prediction and entity coreference resolution. The motivation is to allow the two tasks to influence and mutually benefit from each other.

Sentence distance feature We hypothesize that recency plays a role in resolution, so we add the utterance distance between two spans as an extra feature into $\phi(x, y)$ in UTD^{2021}.

Span speaker constraint UTD^{2021} enforces a constraint on spans that is empirically derived from the training and development data: a span cannot cover more than one speaker's utterance.

Resolution constraint UTD^{2021} enforces a consistency constraint on resolution that will be used in both training and inference. This constraint uses simple heuristics designed for conversations to prevent two spans x and y from being posited as coreferent if they are *conflicting*. More specifically, we check whether a span belongs to one of the following eight groups:

1. span is or starts with: I, me, my, mine
2. span is or starts with: you, your, yours
3. span is or starts with: he, him, his
4. span is or starts with: she, her
5. span is: their
6. span is: it, its
7. span is: here
8. span is: there

Three constraints are applied to spans that belong to these groups:

C1 When two spans have the same speaker: if both of them are from groups 1, 2, 3, or 4 but they are not from the same group, then they cannot be coreferent.

C2 When two spans have different speakers: if both of them are from groups 1 or 2 and they are from the same group, then they cannot be coreferent.

C3 Regardless of the speakers: (1) *here* cannot be coreferent with *my*, *your*, *his*, *her*. and anything in group 5, group 6, and group 8; and (2) *there* cannot be coreferent with *my*, *your*, *his*, *her*, and anything in group 5, group 6, and group 7.

2.3 Our Approach

This year we develop a model for the Anaphora Resolution track that employs a three-step pipelined approach, which is composed of (1) mention extraction; (2) coreference resolution; and (3) removal of non-entity and non-referring mentions.

2.3.1 Step 1: Mention Extraction

The first step of our pipelined approach is to extract entity mentions from documents. As discussed before, $\texttt{UTD}^{2021}$ performs joint entity coreference resolution and type prediction, where type prediction involves predicting each candidate mention span as ENTITY (referring/non-referring spans) or NULL (non-entity spans). We use $\texttt{UTD}^{2021}$ for mention extraction as follows: all and only those candidate mention spans classified as ENTITY will be extracted as entity mentions and processed by the entity coreference model.

Recall that $\texttt{UTD}^{2021}$ employs a loss function that is a weighted sum of the type prediction loss and the entity coreference loss, where the weight is determined by the type loss coefficient. To enable the model to focus on mention extraction (as opposed to entity coreference), we use with a large type loss coefficient. In addition, we disable the resolution constraints when applying $\texttt{UTD}^{2021}$ in this step.

2.3.2 Step 2: Coreference Resolution

The second step of our pipelined approach is to produce coreference links using all and only those spans that are classified as ENTITY in the first step. To achieve this goal, we make the following changes to $\texttt{UTD}^{2021}$ while keeping the span speaker constraint and resolution constraint.

Extracting candidate mention spans Instead of using span enumeration to generate candidate mention spans of up to a predefined length, we use the spans corresponding to gold entity mentions (including both referring or non-referring entity mentions) as the candidate mention spans during training and the spans corresponding to the mentions extracted in the first step as the candidate mention spans during testing.

Removing the type prediction model The type prediction model is no longer needed since the candidate mention spans are either gold spans (during training) or spans extracted in the first step (during testing). Hence, we simply remove it.

Removing the mention score Recall that in `coref-hoi`, the mention score $s_m(\cdot)$ indicates how likely a span corresponds to an entity mention. Since every candidate mention span is either a gold span (during training) or a span extracted in the first step (during testing), the mention score does not play a role anymore in determining how likely two candidate mentions are coreferent. Hence, we remove the mention score from the antecedent-anaphor pairwise score. So the new pairwise score $s(\cdot)$ becomes:

$$s(x, y) = s_c(x, y) + s_a(x, y)$$

where $s_c(\cdot)$ and $s_a(\cdot)$ are the same as those defined in `coref-hoi`.

Inference-time-only dummy antecedent rescoring Recall that in `coref-hoi`, the dummy antecedent is the correct antecedent for non-entity/non-anaphoric mentions. Based on empirical observations on our development data, our resolver fails to select the dummy antecedent as the antecedent for many non-anaphoric mentions. Consequently, we modify the score for dummy antecedents to make the model choose dummy antecedents more frequently. Specifically, instead of having $s(x, \epsilon) = 0$ for dummy antecedents, we make $s(x, \epsilon) = c$ $(c > 0)$ where c is a tunable parameter. By doing this, any candidate antecedent y of span x where $0 < s(x, y) < c$ will not be selected as an antecedent of x.

2.3.3 Step 3: Non-referring/Non-entity Mention Removal

The last step of our pipelined approach is to remove non-entity mentions and non-referring mentions. This step is motivated in part by our observation that our model achieves comparatively low CEAF_e scores on the development data. We hypothesize that this was caused by the large number of erroneously identified singletons that correspond to non-referring or non-entity mentions. To address this problem, we train a model for identifying non-referring and non-entity mentions and apply it to the coreference output produced in Step 2 to remove singleton clusters containing these mentions. Specifically, we reuse our model in the first step, but instead of using span enumeration to generate candidate mention spans, we use gold entity mentions, gold non-referring mentions, and entity mentions in which the underlying word/phrase has appeared at least once as a gold entity mention in the training data as the candidate mention spans. The type prediction model is modified to predict two types: OTHER (for non-referring/non-entity spans) and REFERRING (for referring entity spans). Singletons that are predicted as OTHER are removed from the output.

2.4 Evaluation

In this subsection, we discuss some implementation details and the evaluation results of our system.

2.4.1 Corpora

We mainly use the given ARRAU 3.0 dataset (Uryupina et al., 2019), which contains two text corpora, RST and GNOME, and seven dialogue corpora, TRAINS91, TRAINS93, PEAR, LIGHT, AMI, Persuasion, and Switchboard. Each of the LIGHT, AMI, Persuasion, and Switchboard datasets contains a training set and a development set. Besides ARRAU, we use OntoNotes 5.0[1] to pretrain some of our models. We provide details about how we use these datasets in Section 2.4.2.

2.4.2 Implementation Details

We use SpanBERT$_{\text{Large}}$ as the encoder in all steps. We use different learning rates for the BERT-parameters and the task-parameters (1×10^{-5} and 3×10^{-4} respectively). In all three steps we train the model for 30 epochs with a dropout rate of 0.3. Each document in the training set is split into one or more training instances. Each training instance has at most five continuous segments, each of which contains 512 token pieces. We set n (the top span ratio) to 0.4 and k, the number of candidate antecedents for each candidate anaphor, to 50.

Prior to training on the shared task datasets, we pretrain both the first- and second-step models on OntoNotes 5.0. We do not pretrain our third-step model on OntoNotes because it covers only a portion of non-referring expressions. In fact, the only non-referring expressions covered by OntoNotes 5.0 are the predicate noun phrases, while we have a lot more in the shared task datasets (e.g., expletives, non-referring quantifiers, idioms).

[1]`https://catalog.ldc.upenn.edu/LDC2013T19`

2.4.3 Parameter Tuning

We divide the model parameters into two groups: those to be tuned on the development data and those to be tuned on the test data, as described below.[2]

Parameters tuned on the development data The set of parameters we tune on the development sets includes:

- the span width for span enumeration in the first step: we experiment with span widths out of {5, 10, 30};
- the number of epochs for pretraining the first- and second-step models: we search out of {10, 15, 20};
- the type loss coefficients (for the first- and third-step models): both type loss coefficients are searched out of {0.5, 1, 10, 100, 500, 800};
- the number of training epochs (for all models): we save a model checkpoint every five epochs and use the saved models to perform inference.

Parameters tuned on the test data In our final submissions, all development sets are also used as training data. The set of parameters we tune on the test set (using the model trained on both the training and development data) includes:

- the inference-time-only dummy antecedent re-scoring score (for the second-step model only): we experiment with integer scores between 0 and 10.
- the number of training epochs[3] (for all models): we save a model checkpoint every five epochs. Saved model checkpoints are used to do inference on test sets and inference output is evaluated by making a submission to the shared task competition.

Parameter tuning proceeds as follows. We tune the parameters associated with the three models in our pipeline in a *sequential* manner. Specifically, we first tune the parameters associated with the

[2]In principle, we are not supposed to tune parameters on the test data. We are effectively just exploiting the fact that we can evaluate our models on the test data by submitting our results to the submission site. While we could have tuned all the parameters on the test data, we did not do so because (1) it would take a lot of time to do so and (2) there is a limit on the number of submissions.

[3]Note that the number of training epochs is a parameter that appears in both groups: this parameter is first tuned on the development data and subsequently on the test data.

first-step model. Given the best parameter combination obtained for the first-step model, we then tune the parameters associated with the second-step model. Finally, given the best parameter combination obtained for the models in the first two steps, we tune the parameters associated with the third-step model.

Next, we describe how the parameters associated with each of the three models are tuned. For the first-step model, we first jointly tune the four development-set parameters. Then, using the max span width, the # of epochs for pretraining, and type loss coefficient obtained via this tuning process, we retrain the first-step model on the combined training and development data, tuning the number of training epochs on the test data.

Given the parameters tuned for the first-step model, we tune the parameters in the second-step model. As in the first-step model, we first jointly tune the four development-set parameters in the second-step model, then retrain the model using the best parameter combination on the combined training and development data, tuning the number of training epochs on the test data (assuming a dummy antecedent re-scoring score of 0). Finally, we tune the dummy antecedent re-scoring score.

Finally, given the parameters tuned for the models in the first two steps, we tune the parameters in the third-step model. The parameter tuning process for the third step model is the same as that for the first-step model.

2.4.4 System Variants

So far we have presented our coreference resolver as a three-step pipelined approach. In our evaluation, however, we test the following four variants of our approach:

1. `S1` corresponds to our model without the last two steps. In other words, we use only the first-step model to produce entity coreference results. Note that while the first-step model is intended for mention extraction, it performs joint type prediction and entity coreference resolution and therefore can be used to produce entity coreference results.
2. `S1,S2` corresponds to our model without the third step (removal of non-entity and non-referring mentions from the coreference output).
3. `S1,S3` corresponds to the setup where the coreference output produced by the first-step model is postprocessed by the third-step model to remove non-entity and non-referring mentions; and
4. `S1,S2,S3` is our full model.

	LIGHT	AMI	Pers.	Swbd.
`S1`	78.52	59.56	76.43	72.42
`S1,S2`	79.01	60.64	76.81	71.68
`S1,S3`	81.40	61.51	78.69	**75.81**
`S1,S2,S3`	**82.23**	**62.90**	**79.20**	75.25

Table 2: Anaphora resolution: evaluation results of the four variants of our approach expressed in terms of CoNLL score on the four test sets. The boldfaced results are our strongest results on the four test sets and hence our final results on the shared task competition leaderboard.

2.4.5 Results and Discussion

In this subsection, we report evaluation results obtained by making submissions to the shared task competition, which employs the Universal Anaphora Scorer[4] to calculate the CoNLL score, which is the unweighted average of the F-scores computed using the MUC, B^3, and $CEAF_e$ metrics.

Table 2 shows the entity coreference results on the official test data for the aforementioned four variants of our approach. A few points deserve mention. First, the `S1,S3` variant achieves the best result on Switchboard, while the `S1,S2,S3` variant achieves the best results on the remaining three test sets. Second, by comparing `S1` and `S1,S2`, we can see that `S2` yields only minor improvements (at most 1% CoNLL score) on three datasets and even adversely affects performance on Switchboard. We attribute the ineffectiveness of `S2` to the fact that `S1` has already produced good coreference links for the mentions it extracted. Thus, merely altering the coreference links would not bring much performance improvement. Third, by comparing `S1` and `S1,S3`, we can see that `S3` brings a 2%-3% CoNLL score improvement on all three datasets, which pinpoints one of the weaknesses of `S1` – having too many non-referring/non-mention spans in its prediction. The same conclusion can be drawn for `S2` by comparing `S1,S2` and `S1,S2,S3`.

Detailed evaluation results of the best performing system variant on each dataset in terms of MUC, B^3, and $CEAF_e$ precision (P), recall (R), and F-score (F) are shown in Table 3. As can be seen, the

[4]`https://github.com/juntaoy/universal-anaphora-scorer`

	MUC			B^3			$CEAF_e$			
	P	R	F	P	R	F	P	R	F	CoNLL
LIGHT	90.56	86.86	88.67	80.41	82.43	81.41	73.11	80.45	76.60	82.23
AMI	74.08	66.15	69.89	62.43	63.60	63.01	48.10	66.43	55.80	62.90
Persuasion	88.41	83.67	85.97	78.99	81.23	80.10	64.89	79.70	71.54	79.20
Switchboard	90.14	74.64	81.66	80.92	73.77	77.18	62.20	76.42	68.58	75.81

Table 3: Anaphora resolution: detailed evaluation results on the four test sets. These results are obtained using the system variant that achieves the best result on each test set.

(a) Official CoNLL scores of the system variants.

	`S1`				`S1,S2`				`S1,S2,S3`			
configuration	LIGHT	AMI	Pers.	Swbd.	LIGHT	AMI	Pers.	Swbd.	LIGHT	AMI	Pers.	Swbd.
$\texttt{best}_{\texttt{dev}}$	77.95	58.99	75.71	71.79	78.63	59.18	76.33	71.46	82.18	62.72	79.02	74.86
$\texttt{best}_{\texttt{test}}$	78.52	59.56	76.43	72.42	78.80	60.64	76.72	71.68	-	-	-	-
$\texttt{best}_{\texttt{test}}\texttt{+DR}$	-	-	-	-	79.01	60.64	76.81	71.68	82.23	62.90	79.20	75.25

(b) Parameter settings for each system variant in different configurations.

		`S1`				`S1,S2`				`S1,S2,S3`			
configuration	parameter	LIGHT	AMI	Pers.	Swbd.	LIGHT	AMI	Pers.	Swbd.	LIGHT	AMI	Pers.	Swbd.
$\texttt{best}_{\texttt{dev}}$	Maximum span width	30	30	30	30	-	-	-	-	-	-	-	-
	# of epochs for pretraining	15	15	15	15	15	15	15	15	-	-	-	-
	Type loss coefficient	500	500	500	500	-	-	-	-	500	500	500	500
	# of training epochs	15	15	15	15	10	20	10	5	5	5	10	10
$\texttt{best}_{\texttt{test}}$	Maximum span width	30	30	30	30	-	-	-	-	-	-	-	-
	# of epochs for pretraining	15	15	15	15	15	15	15	15	-	-	-	-
	Type loss coefficient	500	500	500	500	-	-	-	-	-	-	-	-
	# of training epochs	10	20	20	10	15	15	25	25	-	-	-	-
$\texttt{best}_{\texttt{test}}\texttt{+DR}$	Maximum span width	-	-	-	-	-	-	-	-	-	-	-	-
	# of epochs for pretraining	-	-	-	-	15	15	15	15	-	-	-	-
	Type loss coefficient	-	-	-	-	-	-	-	-	500	500	500	500
	# of training epochs	-	-	-	-	15	15	25	25	20	30	5	25
	Dummy antecedent re-scoring	-	-	-	-	3	0	1	0	-	-	-	-

Table 4: Anaphora resolution: official CoNLL scores and detailed parameter settings of three system variants.

performance on AMI is much worse than the performance on any other datasets. We speculate that the poor performance on AMI is related to its comparatively longer documents, as long dependencies are hard for the model to learn.

To better understand the impact of parameter tuning on the resolution performance of the system variants, we report in Tables 4a and 4b the official CoNLL scores and parameter settings for three configurations:

- $\texttt{best}_{\texttt{dev}}$ corresponds to the configuration that yields the highest CoNLL score on the test data when only the development-set parameters are tuned;
- $\texttt{best}_{\texttt{test}}$ corresponds to the configuration that yields the highest CoNLL score on the test data when the development-set parameters and one of the test-set parameters (the number of training epochs) are tuned; and
- $\texttt{best}_{\texttt{test}}\texttt{+DR}$ corresponds to the configuration that yields the hgihest CoNLL score on the test data when the development-set parameters and both of the test-set parameters are tuned. Note that $\texttt{best}_{\texttt{test}}\texttt{+DR}$ and $\texttt{best}_{\texttt{test}}$ differ only in terms of whether the dummy antecedent re-scoring constant is tuned after all the remaining parameters are tuned.

Table 4b reports the parameters as follows. First, the parameters reported for `S1`, `S1,S2`, and `S1,S2,S3` are the parameters obtained for the first-step model, the second-step model, and the third-step model, respectively. Since the parameter associated with these three models are tuned in a sequential fashion, the full set of parameters for `S1,S2,S3` can be recovered from the table by combining parameters from S1, S1,S2, and S1,S2,S3. Second, the first three rows for the three configurations are the same, as those parameters are tuned on the development data only. Third, $\texttt{best}_{\texttt{test}}$+DR for S1 is not applicable, as dummy antecedent re-scoring is used in the second-step model. Moreover, we do not report the results of S1,S3 in this table. Because of time limitations we do not perform parameter tuning for this variant: for the parameters associated with S1 we simply reuse the parameters we tuned for the S1 variant, and for the parameters associated with S3 we set the type loss coefficient to 500 and the number of training epochs to 10.

Several observations can be made on the results in Table 4.[5] First, $\texttt{best}_{\texttt{test}}$ outperforms $\texttt{best}_{\texttt{dev}}$ consistently for a 0.2-1% in CoNLL score, showing that parameter tuning on the test data does lead to performance improvements. Second, dummy antecedent re-scoring is not very effective in improving resolution performance. Comparing $\texttt{best}_{\texttt{test}}$ and $\texttt{best}_{\texttt{test}}$+DR for our S1,S2 model, we see that dummy antecedent re-scoring brings only a diminutive CoNLL score improvement of 0.1-0.2% on two test sets and no improvement at all on the remaining two.

We conclude this section by mentioning that while our systems ranked first among all participants in the anaphora resolution track, there are still some weaknesses in our systems. First, our systems have a hard time handling long dependencies, which we hypothesize to be the main reason why our systems performed the worst on AMI. Second, our system cannot handle cases of plural anaphoric reference in which the antecedents are introduced by separate mentions, namely split antecedents.

3 Discourse Deixis Resolution

The Discourse Deixis track in this year's shared task has three evaluation phases: (1) the Predicted phase, where a system needs to extract both antecedents and anaphors and perform discourse deixis resolution; (2) the Gold Mention phase, which is the same as the Predicted phase except that anaphors are to be extracted from the given set of gold mentions; and (3) the Gold Anaphor phase, which is the same as the Gold Mention phase except that gold anaphors are explicitly given. The Gold Anaphor phase is introduced in this year's shared task to partially address the difficulty of comparing different resolvers with respect to their *resolution* performance (Li et al., 2021).

3.1 Approach

We cast discourse deixis resolution as identity anaphora resolution. This allows us to use Xu and Choi's (2020) coref-hoi model as our baseline for discourse deixis resolution. In this section, we describe our approach to discourse deixis resolution, which is composed of six extensions to coref-hoi.

1. Candidate Anaphor Extraction In the shared task datasets, most deictic expressions are demonstrative pronouns (e.g., "that", "this") and "it". These three pronouns account for more than 80% of the anaphors in the given datasets. Thus, we impose a simple heuristic to extract candidate anaphors: instead of extracting them by span enumeration, we only allow a span in which the underlying word/phrase has appeared at least once in the training set to be a candidate anaphor.

2. Anaphor Prediction Similar to our discourse deixis resolution system in the CODI-CRAC 2021 shared task (Kobayashi et al., 2021), we use a type prediction model in our system this year. Different from last year, however, the type prediction model is used to identify those candidate anaphors that correspond to deictic expressions. Thus, only two types are used: ANAPHOR (the candidate anaphor is indeed a deictic expression) and NULL (the candidate anaphor is not).

3. Candidate Antecedent Extraction Since the shared task datasets are annotated in a way so that only utterances can serve as an antecedent of deictic expressions, we extract candidate antecedents as follows. For each span i that is predicted as ANAPHOR by the type prediction model, we select the 10 utterances that are closest to i (including the utterance in which i appears) as its candidate antecedents. The motivations are that (1) deictic expressions are anaphoric expressions, and hence recency plays an important role in antecedent selection, and (2) using the 10 closest utterances allows us to cover more than 95% of the antecedent-anaphor pairs in the datasets.

4. Dummy Antecedent Elimination In coref-hoi, the set of candidate antecedents for every span includes a dummy antecedent, which

[5] In Table 4a the $\texttt{best}_{\texttt{test}}$ results for S1,S2,S3 are not available due to time limitations.

Type	Features
Anaphor	Embedding of the sentence the anaphor is in
Antecedent	# of words; # of nouns; # of verbs; # of adjectives; # of content word overlaps between antecedent and the preceding words of the anaphor; whether an antecedent is the longest among all candidate antecedents; whether an antecedent has the most content word overlap among all candidate antecedents
Pairwise	Sentence distance between a candidate antecedent and an anaphor, ignoring sentences that contain only interjections, filling words, reporting verbs, and punctuation

Table 5: Additional features used in our model.

will be selected as the antecedent of a span i if (1) i is not an entity mention or (2) i is an entity mention but it is not anaphoric.

For our model, the situation is different. Since only those spans predicted as ANAPHOR by the anaphor prediction model will be passed to the antecedent selection model, the antecedent selection model only sees spans that have been classified as anaphoric. Since these spans are anaphoric, they should presumably not be resolved to the dummy antecedent. For this reason, we eliminate the dummy antecedent from the set of candidate antecedents of every span when training and testing the antecedent selection model.

5. Features Our next extension involves a large-scale expansion of features, hypothesizing that hand-engineered features could be profitably used by a span-based model. Specifically, we incorporate three types of features: (1) anaphor-based features, which encode the context of an anaphor, (2) antecedent-based features, which encode some statistics computed based on a candidate antecedent, and (3) pairwise features, which encode the relationship between an anaphor and a candidate antecedent. The list of features is shown in Table 5. We add these features to both the bilinear score $s_c(x, y)$ and the concatenation-based score $s_a(x, y)$:

$$s_c(x, y) = g_x^\top W_c g_y + g_s^\top W_s g_y$$
$$s_a(x, y) = \mathrm{FFNN}_c(g_x, g_y, g_x \circ g_y, g_s, \phi(x, y))$$

where W_c and W_s are learned weight matrices, g_s is the embedding of the sentence s in which anaphor x appears, and $\phi(x, y)$ encodes the speaker information as well as different types of distance between x and y.

6. Inference-Time-Only Distance-Based Candidate Antecedent Filtering Given that we have fewer training instances for those antecedent-anaphor pairs that have larger sentence distances and it is generally harder to learn long-distance dependencies, correctly resolving an anaphor whose antecedent is far away from it is by no means easy. Although we use only the 10 closest utterances during training, we propose to further lower this number during inference. Specifically, for each candidate anaphor, the model selects an antecedent from one of the n closest utterances ($1 \leq n < 10$), where n is a tunable parameter.

3.2 Evaluation

In this subsection, we evaluate our system and discuss the implementation details.

3.2.1 Implementation Details

The models we use in the three evaluation phases are similar. Specifically, the only difference between our models in different phases lies in Extension 1 (candidate anaphor extraction). In the Predicted phase, candidate anaphors are selected using the method stated in Extension 1. In the Gold Mention phase, the candidate anaphors used for both training and inference are those words/phrases in the given set of gold mentions that appeared in the training set as deictic expressions. In the Gold Anaphor phase, we use the given anaphors for both training and inference, so there is no need to extract anaphors.

We use SpanBERT$_{\text{Large}}$ as the encoder for all evaluation phases. We use different learning rates for the BERT-parameters and the task-parameters (1×10^{-5} and 3×10^{-4} respectively). Each document in the training set is split into one or more training instances. Each training instance has at most 12 continuous segments, each of which contains 512 tokens. Models are trained for 30 epochs with a dropout rate of 0.3.

Note that the models used for the later phases were retrained given the gold mentions and gold anaphors.

3.2.2 Parameter Tuning

Given that we can make submissions to the shared task competition and the amount of data we have is far from abundant, we use all the given datasets as our training set, and tune the following three parameters on the test data (by submitting the system output to the shared task competition):

	MUC			B^3			$CEAF_e$			
	P	R	F	P	R	F	P	R	F	CoNLL
					Predicted Phase					
Light	37.04	31.25	33.90	50.80	33.43	40.32	60.77	26.65	37.05	37.09
AMI	51.67	52.54	52.10	58.76	51.75	55.04	65.06	44.41	52.79	53.31
Persuasion	48.44	59.05	53.22	56.38	57.10	56.74	62.34	47.34	53.82	54.59
Switchboard	63.77	41.12	50.00	70.62	39.28	50.48	76.52	35.82	48.79	49.76
					Gold Mention Phase					
Light	37.17	32.81	34.85	51.59	35.53	42.08	59.81	28.07	38.21	38.38
AMI	54.46	51.69	53.04	63.15	51.87	56.96	69.31	46.07	55.35	55.12
Persuasion	50.00	58.10	53.74	58.16	56.15	57.13	64.52	46.14	53.80	54.89
Switchboard	66.67	42.99	52.27	71.08	39.35	50.65	72.29	34.35	46.57	49.83
					Gold Anaphor Phase					
Light	46.88	46.88	46.88	65.13	50.56	56.93	77.02	40.88	53.41	52.40
AMI	71.19	71.19	71.19	81.05	69.12	74.61	87.47	60.76	71.71	72.50
Persuasion	67.62	67.62	67.62	80.42	67.30	73.28	87.10	55.68	67.93	69.61
Switchboard	70.09	70.09	70.09	80.03	69.83	74.58	86.36	61.25	71.67	72.11

Table 6: Discourse deixis resolution: official results on the test sets.

- the type loss coefficient: we search out of {0.5, 1, 5, 10, 100, 500, 800} using grid search.
- the inference-time-only candidate antecedent filtering constant: we experiment with all integers between 1 and 10.
- the number of training epochs: we save a model checkpoint every five epochs and evaluate it on the test set.

We jointly tune the type loss coefficient and the number of training epochs, and determine the candidate antecedent filtering constant after the other two parameters are fixed.

3.2.3 Results and Discussion

We report the detailed official evaluation results of our system for different phases in Table 6. A few points deserve mention. First, by comparing the results in the Predicted phase and the Gold Mention phase, we can see that even though the set of candidate anaphors is being narrowed down in the Gold Mention phase, only a small performance gain (at most 1% CoNLL score) is achieved. We speculate that our simple heuristic for selecting candidate anaphors is effective, so the provision of gold mentions does not eliminate many plausible candidate anaphors. Second, the provision of gold anaphors has brought huge improvements (14%-22% CoNLL score) to our system, which shows that one of the key weaknesses of our system is anaphor identification. Third, across all three phases, our system performs much worse on LIGHT than on other datasets. Further investigations are needed to determine the reason.

To better understand the impact of parameter tuning on the test data, we show in Tables 7a and 7b the CoNLL scores achieved by three system configurations on the test data:

- $\texttt{worst}_{\texttt{test}}$ corresponds to the configuration that yields the worst result on the test data when only the number of training epochs and the type loss coefficient are jointly tuned (i.e., the antecedent filtering constant is simply set to 10);
- $\texttt{best}_{\texttt{test}}$ corresponds to the configuration that yields the best result on the test data when only the number of training epochs and the type loss coefficient are jointly tuned (i.e., the antecedent filtering constant is simply set to 10);
- $\texttt{best}_{\texttt{test}}\texttt{+AF}$ corresponds to the configuration that yields the best result on the test data when the inference-time-only antecedent filtering constant is tuned, with the other two parameters taken from $\texttt{best}_{\texttt{test}}$.

Several observations can be made on the results shown in Table 7. First, $\texttt{best}_{\texttt{test}}$ outperforms $\texttt{worst}_{\texttt{test}}$ consistently for at most 8% in terms of CoNLL score. The biggest performance gap of 7.97% is observed on the Switchboard test set in the Gold Mention phase: as can be seen, the parameters associated with the two configurations differ only with respect to the number of training epochs. This suggests that the number of epochs plays an important role in the performance of our discourse deixis resolver. Similar conclusions can be drawn by comparing the results in other phases and on other test sets. Second, inference-time-only antecedent filtering generally offers little perfor-

(a) Official CoNLL scores of our models.

	Predicted Phase				Gold Mention Phase				Gold Anaphor Phase			
configuration	LIGHT	AMI	Pers.	Swbd.	LIGHT	AMI	Pers.	Swbd.	LIGHT	AMI	Pers.	Swbd.
worst$_{test}$	34.58	47.36	48.78	45.67	34.07	47.68	49.47	41.86	51.77	68.65	66.78	69.26
best$_{test}$	37.09	51.48	50.30	47.96	37.89	55.12	53.40	49.83	52.40	72.50	69.61	72.11
best$_{test}$+AF	37.09	51.61	50.42	47.96	38.38	55.12	54.89	49.83	52.40	72.50	69.61	72.11

(b) Parameter settings for each setup in different phases.

		Predicted Phase				Gold Mention Phase				Gold Anaphor Phase			
configuration	parameter	LIGHT	AMI	Pers.	Swbd.	LIGHT	AMI	Pers.	Swbd.	LIGHT	AMI	Pers.	Swbd.
worst$_{test}$	Type loss coefficient	0.5	0.5	0.5	0.5	500	100	0.5	500	800	800	800	800
	# of training epochs	10	10	15	10	5	15	15	5	10	15	20	15
	Antecedent filtering constant	10	10	10	10	10	10	10	10	10	10	10	10
best$_{test}$	Type loss coefficient	0.5	0.5	0.5	0.5	800	500	500	500	800	800	800	800
	# of training epochs	10	5	20	20	15	10	10	15	15	5	15	10
	Antecedent filtering constant	10	10	10	10	10	10	10	10	10	10	10	10
best$_{test}$+AF	Type loss coefficient	0.5	0.5	0.5	0.5	800	500	500	500	800	800	800	800
	# of training epochs	10	5	20	20	15	10	10	15	15	5	15	10
	Antecedent filtering constant	10	7	7	10	7	10	7	10	10	10	10	10

Table 7: Discourse deixis resolution: official CoNLL scores of our models and detailed parameter settings in different phases.

mance improvement, though it has yielded performance gains of 0.2%-1.3% in CoNLL score on some test sets.

We conclude this section by pointing out that our system ranked first for all three phases in the discourse deixis resolution track. While our system was 1%-5% CoNLL scores better than the second-ranked team in the Predicted phase and the Gold mention phase, our system outperformed the second-ranked team by large margins of 5%-16% CoNLL scores in the Gold Anaphor phase, which shows the effectiveness of our system in discourse deixis resolution.

4 Bridging Resolution

Like the Discourse Deixis track, the Bridging Resolution track in this year's shared task has three different phases, namely the Predicted phase, the Gold Mention phase, and the Gold Anaphor phase. While discourse deixis resolution has received fairly little attention in the NLP community in recent years, constant progress has been made for bridging resolution. Nevertheless, such progress has thus far limited to a large extent to the Gold Mention setting, where gold mentions are given, and the Gold Anaphor setting, where gold anaphors are given (see Kobayashi and Ng (2020) for a comprehensive overview and Kobayashi et al. (2022a) for state-of-the-art results). In particular, little progress has been made on end-to-end bridging resolution, which corresponds to the setup used in the Predicted phase of the shared task.

Motivated in part by the success of the hybrid rule-based and learning-based approach to bridging resolution developed by Kobayashi and Ng (2021), we adopted a multi-pass sieve approach to bridging resolution in last year's shared task, where we employed a pipeline of sieves consisting of a neural sieve, which is essentially Yu and Poesio's span-based neural model that employs multi-task learning, and a set of same-head sieves, which were specifically designed to target the identification of bridging links between two mentions having the same head. Given that the improvement offered by the same-head sieves is small, we abandon them this year and focus instead on extending Yu and Poesio's multi-task learning framework for bridging resolution. Below we first provide an overview of Yu and Poesio's model.

4.1 Yu and Poesio's (2020) Model

Yu and Poesio's (Y&P) model is a span-based neural model that takes gold mentions as input and jointly performs entity coreference resolution and bridging resolution. The way Y&P differs from other end-to-end span-based coreference models is that it uses two FFNN's to separately predict coreference links and bridging links. These two FFNNs share the first few hidden layers as well as the span representation layer. The loss function of this MTL model is composed of a weighted sum of the losses of the bridging task and the coreference task. Unlike feature-based approaches to bridging resolution, where feature engineering plays a critical role in performance, this neural model employs only two features, the length of a mention and the mention-pair distance.

4.2 Approach

Since Y&P's model takes gold mentions as input, we need a mention extractor before we can deploy it. For this reason, we employ a pipelined approach to bridging resolution, where we first extract mentions using a mention extractor and then perform bridging resolution using our extended Y&P model. Below we describe the extensions we made to Y&P.

4.2.1 Extensions to the Y&P Model

We employ two extensions to the Y&P model.

Using SpanBERT as encoder Given the successful application of SpanBERT to entity coreference in the past few years, it is natural to think about applying SpanBERT to bridging resolution. In fact, SpanBERT has recently been shown to yield promising results when applied to resolving bridging references in narratives (Kobayashi et al., 2022b). Hence, our first extension to Y&P involves replacing its biLSTM encoder and the frozen BERT/Glove embeddings used by the biLSTM with $\text{SpanBERT}_{\text{Large}}$ in order to strengthen Y&P's performance. We adopt the independent version of Joshi et al. (2019), where each input document is split into non-overlapping segments of length up to L_s.

Adding Turn Distance as a feature As mentioned above, Y&P employs only two features, namely the length of a mention and the mention-pair distance. Since Y&P is not designed for the dialogue domain, neither of the two features captures information regarding the dialogue domain. We follow our work in last year's shared task and add the turn distance between mentions as a feature, where a turn is defined as a set of contiguous sentences by the same speaker.

4.3 Evaluation

In this subsection, we evaluate our system and discuss the implementation details.

4.3.1 Implementation Details

Each document is split into segments of length 384. The 40% top scoring spans are retained for bridging resolution. The weight parameter associated with the weighted sum of losses of the bridging task and the coreference task is set to 1, meaning that the two tasks are given equal importance in the learning process. Below we discuss how the models used for the three phases differ from each other.

4.3.1.1 Predicted Phase

In the Predicted phase, our system needs to extract mentions and perform bridging resolution. We first use our `S1` system described in Section 2 to extract mentions, then use our modified Y&P model to perform bridging resolution on the extracted mentions.

We test our model with the following training setups as different setups may lead to large performance differences:

- `T1`: In this setup, we use all the available datasets for model training, namely ARRAU RST, GNOME, TRAINS91, TRAINS93, LIGHT, AMI, Persuasion, and Switchboard. In particular, both the training split and the development split of LIGHT, AMI, Persuasion, and Switchboard are used for training. Our system is trained for at most 25 epochs.
- `T2`: In this setup, we first pretrain our system on the datasets that are outside of the target (i.e., dialogue) domain, namely ARRAU RST, GNOME, TRAINS91, and TRAINS93, for 15 epochs. After that, we train our system on one dataset that contains all of the data from the target domain, namely LIGHT, AMI, Persuasion, and Switchboard, for 25 epochs.
- `T3`: Similar to `T2`, we first pretrain our system on the datasets that are outside of the target domain for 15 epochs. However, for each dataset from the target domain, we train our model for 25 epochs using both the training split and the development split of that target domain. For instance, when evaluating our system on $\text{LIGHT}_{\text{test}}$, we train a model on $\text{LIGHT}_{\text{train}}$ and $\text{LIGHT}_{\text{dev}}$. Hence, the documents used to train the models in `T3` are a subset of those used to train the models in `T2`.

In preliminary experiments, we found that models trained with both predicted mentions and gold mentions performed better than models trained with only gold mentions. Thus, for each training setup, we first extract mentions from the training

		Light			AMI			Persuasion			Switchboard		
		P	R	F	P	R	F	P	R	F	P	R	F
Predicted Phase													
Recognition	T1	56.80	26.23	35.89	42.46	17.59	24.88	39.35	35.86	37.52	55.30	25.86	35.24
	T2	53.37	33.13	40.88	37.44	18.29	24.57	41.46	39.14	40.27	46.48	28.45	35.29
	T3	46.20	41.13	43.52	43.87	15.74	23.17	35.09	43.75	38.95	48.93	34.48	40.46
Resolution	T1	34.93	16.13	22.07	22.91	9.49	**13.42**	27.80	25.33	26.51	27.65	12.93	17.62
	T2	30.36	18.84	**23.25**	18.48	9.03	12.13	28.57	26.97	**27.75**	22.89	14.01	17.38
	T3	24.07	21.43	22.67	22.58	8.10	11.93	24.80	30.92	27.53	23.85	16.81	**19.72**
Gold Mention Phase													
Recognition	T1	61.66	23.77	34.31	52.76	24.31	33.28	44.36	40.13	42.14	53.99	18.97	28.07
	T2	57.85	35.84	44.26	43.55	25.00	31.76	46.02	43.75	44.86	49.16	31.47	38.37
	T3	56.04	34.85	42.98	40.38	34.49	37.20	41.27	49.01	44.81	49.44	37.72	42.79
Resolution	T1	39.30	15.15	21.87	31.16	14.35	**19.65**	32.36	29.28	30.74	31.29	10.99	16.27
	T2	34.99	21.67	**26.77**	21.77	12.50	15.88	34.60	32.89	33.73	26.26	16.81	20.50
	T3	33.86	21.06	25.97	18.70	15.97	17.23	31.86	37.83	**34.59**	26.27	20.04	**22.74**
Gold Anaphor Phase													
Recognition	T1	97.78	97.78	97.78	97.69	97.69	97.69	98.03	98.03	98.03	98.49	98.49	98.49
	T2	97.78	97.78	97.78	97.69	97.69	97.69	98.03	98.03	98.03	98.49	98.49	98.49
	T4	97.78	97.78	97.78	97.69	97.69	97.69	98.03	98.03	98.03	98.49	98.49	98.49
Resolution	T1	46.80	46.80	**46.80**	39.35	39.35	**39.35**	56.58	56.58	56.58	43.75	43.75	43.75
	T2	40.15	40.15	40.15	31.71	31.71	31.71	51.97	51.97	51.97	37.07	37.07	37.07
	T4	46.55	46.55	46.55	38.19	38.19	38.19	56.91	56.91	**56.91**	44.40	44.40	**44.40**

Table 8: Bridging resolution: recognition results and resolution results on the test sets. The boldfaced results are the official F-scores of our system on the shared task leaderboard.

set using our `S1` system[6] and then use the extracted mentions along with the gold mentions for model training.

4.3.1.2 Gold Mention Phase

In the Gold Mention phase, we do not retrain our models. Instead, we perform bridging resolution on the given gold mentions in the test data using the models trained in the Predicted phase.

4.3.1.3 Gold Anaphor Phase

In the Gold Anaphor phase, since gold anaphors are explicitly given, we constrain our models so that only gold anaphors can be resolved to other gold mentions during both training and inference. We test our models using the `T1` and `T2` setups mentioned in Section 4.3.1 as well as a new setup:

`T4`: After training our model in the `T1` setup, we execute an extra fine-tuning step where we fine-tune our model for 25 epochs using both the training split and the development split of the target domain. For instance, when evaluating our system on $\text{LIGHT}_{\text{test}}$, we first train a model using the `T1` setup and then fine-tune the resulting model on $\text{LIGHT}_{\text{train}}$.

`T4` serves as an alternative to `T3`. The only difference between `T3` and `T4` is that `T3` performs fine-tuning on the target domain *after* it finishes pretraining on datasets outside of the target domain, whereas `T4` performs extra fine-tuning on the target domain after a model is trained according to `T1`.

4.3.2 Parameter Tuning

We do not tune any parameters on the development data. The number of training epochs is the only parameter we tune on the test data. As in anaphora resolution and discourse deixis resolution, to tune the number of training epochs we save a model checkpoint every five epochs and evaluate it on the test set. Note that the number of training epochs is tuned separately for each setup.

4.3.3 Results and Discussion

For each test set, the best resolution result achieved over all setups will be used as our official result. Table 8 shows the official recognition and resolution results of our bridging resolver on the test sets. Our system achieves resolution F-scores of 13.42%-27.75% for the Predicted phase. For the Gold Mention phase and Gold Anaphor phase, our

[6] Note that `S1`, which was trained on the training set, is applied to the training set to extract mentions.

(a) Predicted phase

# epochs	T1, Predicted Phase				T2, Predicted Phase				T3, Predicted Phase			
	LIGHT	AMI	Pers.	Swbd.	LIGHT	AMI	Pers.	Swbd.	LIGHT	AMI	Pers.	Swbd.
5	17.44	13.42	24.78	13.46	23.20	10.73	24.78	19.23	22.67	11.93	25.09	17.68
10	17.75	11.98	25.27	15.76	22.24	10.49	26.05	17.12	22.58	11.17	27.53	19.72
15	22.07	13.27	26.51	17.62	23.25	12.13	26.73	17.38	21.48	11.73	26.64	16.16
20	20.61	11.73	24.59	17.54	22.06	11.91	27.75	17.08	22.66	11.24	26.94	16.24
25	21.43	12.48	22.80	17.33	23.12	11.73	27.42	17.26	21.52	10.88	25.65	17.85

(b) Gold Anaphor phase

# epochs	T1, Gold Anaphor Phase				T2, Gold Anaphor Phase				T4, Gold Anaphor Phase			
	LIGHT	AMI	Pers.	Swbd.	LIGHT	AMI	Pers.	Swbd.	LIGHT	AMI	Pers.	Swbd.
5	46.80	37.73	56.58	43.75	38.92	28.47	48.36	32.76	46.55	37.04	53.62	44.40
10	46.31	39.35	48.68	42.67	40.15	31.71	51.32	37.07	46.55	36.11	53.62	42.24
15	45.94	37.04	51.32	42.24	38.55	30.56	50.00	36.21	46.55	37.27	54.93	42.03
20	45.07	37.04	52.63	43.32	36.95	30.79	51.97	35.99	46.55	38.19	56.91	43.10
25	44.83	38.43	52.30	42.46	37.68	29.86	50.33	35.34	-	-	-	-

Table 9: Bridging resolution: official resolution F-scores of our models in terms of the number of training epochs and the setup for two phases.

system achieves F-scores of 19.65%-34.59% and 39.35%-56.91% respectively. The performance improvements in the later phases should not be surprising, as the task becomes progressively easier in the later phases.

A few points deserve mention. First, the results show a strong positive correlation between recognition performance and resolution performance. This should not be surprising either, as strong recognition performance lays the foundation for strong resolution performance. Second, as mentioned above, we do not retrain our models in the Gold Mention phase. Thus, the performance gains we achieve in the Gold Mention phase over the Predicted phase can be attributed solely to the difference between using predicted mentions and using gold mentions. In particular, almost all setups achieve better performance in the Gold Mention phase except T1 on Switchboard, where worse results are obtained for both recognition and resolution performance. We speculate that, although gold mentions are given, identifying bridging anaphors is still a non-trivial task. Additional experiments are needed to determine the reason, however. Third, in the Gold Anaphor phase, all setups achieve much better results than those in the Gold Mention phase. In some setups the results increase by 100%. This should not be surprising, as anaphor recognition performance has gone from around 30% F-score to nearly 100% F-score.

To examine the impact of parameter tuning on the test data, we show in Tables 9a and 9b how the resolution F-score of our bridging resolver on the test data varies with the number of training epochs for each setup. Note that these results are available only for the Predicted phase and the Gold Anaphor phase but not the Gold Mention phase because in the Gold Mention phase we simply reuse the models trained during the Predicted phase. As we can see, the number of training epochs has a large impact on the performance of our bridging resolver: the difference in resolution F-score between the worst combination and the best combination can be as large as 4.63%. The choice of setup can lead to a even larger difference — an F-score difference of 11.64% between T2 and T4 on $\text{Switchboard}_{\text{test}}$ in the Gold Anaphor phase.

We conclude this section by mentioning that our system ranked first in all phases of the bridging resolution track. In particular, our system outperformed the second-ranking team for 4%-9% resolution F-scores in the Gold Anaphor phase.

5 Conclusions

We presented the systems that we developed for all three tracks of the CODI-CRAC 2022 shared task, namely the anaphora resolution track, the bridging resolution track, and the discourse deixis resolution track. For anaphora resolution, we employed a three-step approach consisting of mention extraction, coreference resolution, and removal of non-referring and non-entity mentions. Our results demonstrated that the third-step model, the non-referring/non-entity removal model, contributed a lot to overall resolution performance. However, our system is still not able to handle split-antecedents, which is a direction for future improvements. For discourse deixis resolution, our results revealed that one of the key weaknesses in our system is anaphor detection, as a large performance gain could be achieved when the model was applied to gold anaphors. For bridging resolution, our results showed that the Gold Anaphor phase was much easier than the Predicted phase and the Gold Mention phase. The resulting large performance gap provided suggestive evidence that there is still a lot of room for improvement in bridging anaphor detection. Future work should focus on (1) determining the extent to which performance would deteriorate when all model parameters are tuned on development data and (2) performing a cross-team analysis to better understand how the resolvers from different teams are different from each other.

Acknowledgments

This work was supported in part by NSF Grant IIS-1528037. Any opinions, findings, conclusions or recommendations expressed in this paper are those of the authors and do not necessarily reflect the views or official policies, either expressed or implied, of the NSF.

References

Mandar Joshi, Danqi Chen, Yinhan Liu, Daniel S. Weld, Luke Zettlemoyer, and Omer Levy. 2020. SpanBERT: Improving pre-training by representing and predicting spans. *Transactions of the Association for Computational Linguistics*, 8:64–77.

Mandar Joshi, Omer Levy, Luke Zettlemoyer, and Daniel Weld. 2019. BERT for coreference resolution: Baselines and analysis. In *Proceedings of the 2019 Conference on Empirical Methods in Natural Language Processing and the 9th International Joint Conference on Natural Language Processing (EMNLP-IJCNLP)*, pages 5803–5808, Hong Kong, China. Association for Computational Linguistics.

Sopan Khosla, Juntao Yu, Ramesh Manuvinakurike, Vincent Ng, Massimo Poesio, Michael Strube, and Carolyn Rosé. 2021. The CODI-CRAC 2021 shared task on anaphora, bridging, and discourse deixis in dialogue. In *Proceedings of the CODI-CRAC 2021 Shared Task on Anaphora, Bridging, and Discourse Deixis in Dialogue*, pages 1–15, Punta Cana, Dominican Republic. Association for Computational Linguistics.

Hideo Kobayashi, Yufang Hou, and Vincent Ng. 2022a. Constrained multi-task learning for bridging resolution. In *Proceedings of the 60th Annual Meeting of the Association for Computational Linguistics (Volume 1: Long Papers)*, pages 759–770, Dublin, Ireland. Association for Computational Linguistics.

Hideo Kobayashi, Yufang Hou, and Vincent Ng. 2022b. End-to-end neural bridging resolution. In *Proceedings of the 29th International Conference on Computational Linguistics*, Gyeongju, Republic of Korea. International Committee on Computational Linguistics.

Hideo Kobayashi, Shengjie Li, and Vincent Ng. 2021. Neural anaphora resolution in dialogue. In *Proceedings of the CODI-CRAC 2021 Shared Task on Anaphora, Bridging, and Discourse Deixis in Dialogue*, pages 16–31, Punta Cana, Dominican Republic. Association for Computational Linguistics.

Hideo Kobayashi and Vincent Ng. 2020. Bridging resolution: A survey of the state of the art. In *Proceedings of the 28th International Conference on Computational Linguistics*, pages 3708–3721, Barcelona, Spain (Online). International Committee on Computational Linguistics.

Hideo Kobayashi and Vincent Ng. 2021. Bridging resolution: Making sense of the state of the art. In *Proceedings of the 2021 Conference of the North American Chapter of the Association for Computational Linguistics: Human Language Technologies*, pages 1652–1659, Online. Association for Computational Linguistics.

Kenton Lee, Luheng He, and Luke Zettlemoyer. 2018. Higher-order coreference resolution with coarse-to-fine inference. In *Proceedings of the 2018 Conference of the North American Chapter of the Association for Computational Linguistics: Human Language Technologies, Volume 2 (Short Papers)*, pages 687–692, New Orleans, Louisiana. Association for Computational Linguistics.

Shengjie Li, Hideo Kobayashi, and Vincent Ng. 2021. The CODI-CRAC 2021 shared task on anaphora, bridging, and discourse deixis resolution in dialogue: A cross-team analysis. In *Proceedings of the CODI-CRAC 2021 Shared Task on Anaphora, Bridging, and Discourse Deixis in Dialogue*, pages 71–95, Punta Cana, Dominican Republic. Association for Computational Linguistics.

Jing Lu and Vincent Ng. 2020. Conundrums in entity coreference resolution: Making sense of the state of the art. In *Proceedings of the 2020 Conference on Empirical Methods in Natural Language Processing (EMNLP)*, pages 6620–6631, Online. Association for Computational Linguistics.

Olga Uryupina, Ron Artstein, Antonella Bristot, Federica Cavicchio, Francesca Delogu, Kepa Joseba Rodríguez, and Massimo Poesio. 2019. Annotating a broad range of anaphoric phenomena, in a variety of genres: the ARRAU corpus. *Natural Language Engineering*, 26:95 – 128.

Liyan Xu and Jinho D. Choi. 2020. Revealing the myth of higher-order inference in coreference resolution. In *Proceedings of the 2020 Conference on Empirical Methods in Natural Language Processing (EMNLP)*, pages 8527–8533, Online. Association for Computational Linguistics.

Liyan Xu and Jinho D. Choi. 2021. Adapted end-to-end coreference resolution system for anaphoric identities in dialogues. In *Proceedings of the CODI-CRAC 2021 Shared Task on Anaphora, Bridging, and Discourse Deixis in Dialogue*, pages 55–62, Punta Cana, Dominican Republic. Association for Computational Linguistics.

Juntao Yu, Bernd Bohnet, and Massimo Poesio. 2020. Neural mention detection. In *Proceedings of the 12th Language Resources and Evaluation Conference*, pages 1–10, Marseille, France. European Language Resources Association.

Juntao Yu, Sopan Khosla, Ramesh Manuvinakurike, Lori Levin, Vincent Ng, Massimo Poesio, Michael Strube, and Carolyn Rosé. 2022. The CODI-CRAC 2022 shared task on anaphora, bridging, and discourse deixis in dialogue. In *Proceedings of the CODI-CRAC 2022 Shared Task on Anaphora, Bridging, and Discourse Deixis in Dialogue*, Gyeongju, Republic of Korea. Association for Computational Linguistics.

Juntao Yu and Massimo Poesio. 2020. Multitask learning-based neural bridging reference resolution. In *Proceedings of the 28th International Conference on Computational Linguistics*, pages 3534–3546, Barcelona, Spain (Online). International Committee on Computational Linguistics.

Author Index